DELIVERANCE
TO THE CAPTIVES

works by Karl Barth available in English:

THE WORD OF GOD AND THE WORD OF MAN
THE EPISTLE TO THE ROMANS
CHURCH DOGMATICS
THE KNOWLEDGE OF GOD AND THE SERVICE OF GOD
PRAYER
AGAINST THE STREAM
DOGMATICS IN OUTLINE
THE TEACHING OF THE CHURCH REGARDING BAPTISM
CHRIST AND ADAM
PROTESTANT THOUGHT: From Rousseau to Ritschl
THE FAITH OF THE CHURCH
THE HUMANITY OF GOD
SHORTER COMMENTARY ON ROMANS
ANSELM: *Fides Quaerens Intellectum
(Faith in Search of Understanding)*

Karl Barth

DELIVERANCE
TO THE CAPTIVES

He hath sent me to preach . . .
deliverance to the captives
ST LUKE 4.18

HARPER & BROTHERS
NEW YORK

CONTENTS

PREFACE

By Dr John Marsh, Principal of Mansfield College, Oxford

IT is not given to many men, especially if they be theologians, to stamp their names upon an age. I cannot tell whether in the years to come those who write the history of Christian doctrine will call our century 'The Age of Barth', but I do know that they will write a very inadequate history unless they indicate that none of us alive today can worthily claim the honoured title of theologian unless we have wrestled with the searching questions that Karl Barth has been putting to the Church since 1918.

I first heard of Karl Barth when I was a student of philosophy in the University of Edinburgh. Professor Norman Kemp Smith, one of my wise and revered teachers, urged me in 1929 to read a book which, as he put it, 'will help you to convince your fellow churchmen that Christianity is not just drinking cups of tea with Ladies' Sewing Parties'. The book was Karl Barth's *The Word of God and the Word of Man*.

Since then I have tried to listen to the questions that Barth has addressed to the Church. They have always been deeply theological questions, and yet always profoundly concerned in quite drastic ways with the very life of the Church. The historic Synod at Barmen in 1934 gathered the brave little 'Confessional Church' that took on Hitler and his colleagues as they tried to strangle the Church; and its meeting was very largely due to the fact that Barth had made the Churches of Germany face some most searching and awkward questions about the duty of the Church under a tyrant like Hitler. Barth has never ceased to be able to see and to express the relevance of his profound theology for the contemporary life of the Christian Church.

There is one story about Barth that I shall never forget. I was in Germany in the early days of 1938 on the very day when the second volume of his great *Dogmatik* was delivered in the post of the German Confessional Pastor with whom I was staying. It was as if a year's supply of food had come to some beleaguered city that would otherwise have starved to death. I shall never forget the joy and delight of that morning post; and I have never since been able to give much credence to the critics who, from a safe and comfortable Anglo-American study armchair, tell the world that Barth's theology is theoretical and remote. Theoretical, in one sense, of course it must be, if it be theology at all; but remote, no!—not after I had seen how much his writing was a veritable munition of war in the death struggle of the Church, which was given victory very largely through the writings of Karl Barth.

If I were writing an introduction to a theological work by Karl Barth I would be intrigued to discuss the way in which his views have been received in the Anglo-Saxon world. He has his critics, and many of them find his views preposterous; he has his disciples, and they find his guidance most reliable and—after due hard thinking—highly rewarding. But I suppose that both critics and disciples have often wondered 'How does this theology preach?' And for Barth that would not be a very wrong sort of question, since theology is for him the tool by which we make clear to ourselves and to the world what the content of our preaching means. How does Barth's theology preach? I think the question would be better put: 'What sort of preaching lies behind this kind of theology?' Here is the answer. I have heard many 'Barthians' (though Barth would himself disallow the name) preach, with varying satisfaction. Here the great theologian can be heard himself. In these sermons he speaks mainly to the inmates of a Swiss prison, for while Professor of Theology at Basel University Karl Barth has exercised a truly remarkable hidden ministry, visiting and preaching regularly in Basel Prison. I think this congregation would put any man's theology to the test; for it is not easy to know what to say to men and women in prison, nor how to say it. I cannot think that any will read these sermons without realizing that Barth has a wonderful power to enter into the situation of the audience, and to speak most relevantly to it.

If I were asked to put into one sentence the basic principle that underlies all Barth's theology I think I would say that it is directed, all the way through, to but one end—*to leave completely undistorted and uncompromised the great, wonderful and mysterious fact that God has spoken to us in his Son, Jesus Christ our Lord.* This, as I believe, underlies his insistence upon the transcendence of God, the vanity of reason, the sinfulness and helpfulness of man, the sole sufficiency of God's good grace. If the story that God has spoken to us in his Son is to be told, and told so that it is a real story, a dire necessity if man is to be saved at all, then, so at least Barth believes, all the distinctive and even the 'extreme' emphases of his theology follow. I think that this is very adequately illustrated in the sermons before us.

I have read these sermons through with immense profit, because I could not read them without having to search my own soul, and ask myself some disturbingly awkward but curative questions. I cannot but think that every reader will profit immensely too. If anyone has read Barth's theology and found it difficult to understand or to accept, let him read the sermon entitled 'Saved by grace'; for here is truly evangelical preaching. Barth makes it quite plain that God is very highly exalted, that man is lost, totally and absolutely lost, in sin; that he can do nothing to help himself out of his lost condition; but all that is said, and can only be said, because of the tremendous news of the gospel, that God has spoken a word of salvation, has acted out the drama of our salvation, in Jesus Christ our Lord. And Barth knows that when he preaches to prisoners he is but preaching to himself, to them and to himself as dying sinners and yet as men redeemed from death by the gracious act of God.

There is much that could be said of these sermons: they are in language and essence simple; they are filled with an immense understanding and sympathy; that have a wonderful 'personal' quality; but above all they exalt Christ and show him as the one who in all our sorrow, tragedy and sin, in all our brave struggle to keep ourselves decently moral and religious, is the only hope and the indubitable assurance that in the end what God has designed for us will not be in vain. We can but thank publisher and translator for enabling us to share in the preaching of the gospel in the chapel of a Swiss prison. The gospel has shown that the real prison is in the heart of each one of us, and has offered deliverance to all of us captives. Were it not for that, I should have been envious of those Swiss prisoners!

JOHN MARSH

REMARKS

By the Preacher and the Prison Chaplain

IT is not the task of the preacher of these sermons to write a preface to this book. He can only make a few preliminary remarks.

With a few exceptions, these sermons were preached in the Prison of Basel. Martin Schwarz, the chaplain, had asked me one day to replace him in the pulpit. Over the years, I have been on several occasions a guest in this house church and always enjoyed it. I am very glad that some of its members took it upon themselves to print in their own shop what I had to say.

I should like to add one thing. In preparing and conducting the worship services, the prayers I gave were to my mind as essential as the sermons themselves. I hope that this will hold true in turn for those who, through reading this book, share in these services.

KARL BARTH

When it became widely known that Karl Barth preaches from time to time in the prison of Basel, people reacted in various ways. Some were amazed, others shrugged their shoulders or shook their heads, but the great majority heartily approved. The thought was even ventured that in order to hear Karl Barth preach, one had to break the law and be put in jail. The following questions were foremost in the minds of Christians and non-Christians alike. Are those privileged to listen to these sermons open to their message and grateful for it? Are they duly appreciative of this man's presence in their midst? Do they understand his language? Is it appropriate to proclaim in such a place first the gospel and not the Law? Is an audience made up of prisoners not by nature critical, presumably even not very 'Christian'?

These sermons were indeed preached before avowedly critical and 'un-Christian' people. For this very reason, one is tempted to continue, they were sympathetically heard and understood. Yet the reverse may also be said. Because these sermons expound soberly and joyfully, without any note of hypocrisy, the central affirmations of the Christian faith, therefore they were heard and understood and accepted by this critical, 'un-Christian' audience.

There are many signs that show how through these sermons the strangers within the gate found themselves challenged by the gospel, understood in their guilt and need, comforted and strengthened in their struggle. They made the prayers their own. They not only expressed their gratitude to Karl Barth and loved him; they also joined in the fellowship under the Word and in the joyful celebration of the Lord's Supper following most of these sermons.

MARTIN SCHWARZ

NEVERTHELESS I AM CONTINUALLY WITH THEE

1 August 1954

O Lord our God! We give thee thanks that we may meet in this hour to call on thee, to bring before thee all that troubles us, to hear together the good news of the salvation of the world, to give thee honour and glory.

Come thyself into our midst! Awaken us all! Grant us thy light! Be our teacher and comforter! Speak to each one of us in such a way that we may hear that personal word of help we need.

Show thy mercy to all who are gathered this morning as thy congregation wherever they may be! Keep us and them steadfast in thy word! Keep us and them from hypocrisy, error and distraction! Grant us and them insight and hope, a clear word of witness and joyful hearts! Through Jesus Christ our Lord. Amen.

Nevertheless I am continually with thee; thou dost hold my right hand.

PSALM 73.23

MY DEAR BROTHERS AND SISTERS, for you I will try, briefly, to clarify what we have here. You will see that each word is significant.

'Nevertheless' is the opening word. 'Nevertheless' means 'in spite of'. It stands for defiance. It is a war cry against a threatening power, a dangerous interference or affliction. These take the form perhaps of an almost irreparable loss; perhaps of 'circumstances', as we say, caused by others if not by ourselves in most cases; perhaps of one or more individuals whom we cannot stand because they are in our way; perhaps even of our own personalities, of ourselves such as we are individually.

All of you may have heard or even joined in the song:

Unser Leben gleicht der Reise eines Wandrer's in der Nacht;
Jeder hat auf seinem Gleise etwas, was ihm Kummer macht.

Our life is like the journey of a wanderer through the night;
and each one, advancing slowly, knows: deep sorrow is his
plight.

Each one! Sorrow is your plight, and so it is mine. We suffer here within the walls of this house, and so do the people of this city, even of the whole world. Behind the sorrow of each individual there lies the sorrow of a world in disorder, of a harassed, dark and dangerous world. There also lies the sorrow of man as he is: not good, but haughty and lazy, a liar and a poor wretch, not well off, but living in misery.

What a great thing it would be were we able to throw in the face of all these adversities the defiant 'nevertheless!'

'Nevertheless *I am*' would then mean: in spite of everything I live! I will swim against the stream! I will not give in! I will not despair, I will not drown! Rather, I will persevere and, what is more, I will have confidence and hope! I will keep above water and not be submerged! Truly, he who could freely master his own great and small troubles, and the plight of the world and of mankind, might rejoicingly exclaim: 'Nevertheless *I am*!'

'Nevertheless I am *continually*' implies: at all times and in all circumstances, whatever happens, through thick and thin. Hence, not only occasionally, not only in the morning, but also in the evening when the darkness deepens and the night falls, not only in good times but also in bad times, not only when the good news pour in but also amidst the steady flow of distressing news, even in the grip of disappointment and dejection. As Luther affirms in the hymn you all know:

> And were this world all devils o'er,
> And watching to devour us,
> We lay it not to heart so sore;
> Not they can overpower us.[1]

This is *continually*! What a man he would be who could say, and not merely say but think and experience it: *Nevertheless I am continually!*

Dear brothers and sisters, the Bible where these words are written is one great invitation extended to us all. Whenever we gather for worship, as we do right now, the invitation is addressed to us. As worshippers we can and we may repeat in our hearts: 'Nevertheless I am continually!' *All* of us are invited, the so-called good and the so-called bad, those who are happy and those who believe they are unhappy, the pious and the admittedly less pious if not downright impious folks. Do you realize that the Bible is a *book of freedom*, and that divine worship is a *celebration of freedom*? This is much more important than our beautiful Independence Day, the First of August, which we once again celebrated today in remembrance of 1291! In worship,

[1] From Martin Luther's *Ein' feste Burg*, translated by Thomas Carlyle.

my brothers and sisters, we celebrate the freedom to proclaim that 'nevertheless I am continually'.

But at this point we need to watch out. I would bet 100 to 1 that all of us, were it a matter of choice, would continue: nevertheless I am continually—*with myself*! I stand by my mind, by my opinion, by my point of view, by my rights! I stand by my aims and by my claims! 'Nevertheless I am continually' would thus imply reliance on our own strength in defiance of all and everything. A good friend of mine likes to quote his favourite saying from a poem by the Swiss poet, Leuthold: *Mein stolzes Herz, sei du dir selbst genug* ('My proud heart, be sufficient unto thyself'). Whenever he recites his favourite line I cannot help a chuckle. Such thoughts and such talk cannot be forbidden. We all are wont to such self-confidence at times. But let us get it straight in our minds that this is an impasse. Have you ever seen a dog chasing its own tail? Or heard about the Baron of Muenchhausen pulling himself out of the swamp by his own hair? Nobody believed him. We cannot believe in ourselves, and we cannot hold on to ourselves. For the harassed, the dark and dangerous world lurks in my own 'proud heart'. In what sense could we then say: 'Nevertheless I am continually with myself'? The Bible calls it *sin* when man wants to be with himself. Certainly where this is the case there is no freedom.

In the Bible, the book of freedom, we read differently: 'Nevertheless I am continually *with thee*.' My friends, picture for a moment a man groping in the dark who suddenly sees a light, or another who is starved and suddenly receives a piece of bread, or one who is dying with thirst and is offered a cup of water. This is what happens to us when we leave behind the 'with myself' and break through to the conviction: 'nevertheless I am continually *with thee*.'

What kind of a '*thou*' is this? Is it a *man*? Yes, indeed, someone with a human face, a human body, human hands and a human language. One whose heart bears sorrows—not simply his own, but the sorrows of the whole world. One who takes our sin and our misery upon himself and away from us. One who is able to do this because he is not only man, but also *God*, the almighty Creator and Lord who knows me and you much better than we know ourselves, who loves me and you much more than we love ourselves. He is our neighbour, he is closer to us than we are to ourselves, and we may call him by his first name.

Do you know who he is? The hymn already quoted gives us the answer:

> Christ Jesus is his name,
>   The Lord Sabaoth's Son;
> He, and no other one,
>   Shall conquer in the battle.

Brothers and sisters, we are now all invited to talk to him instead of talking to ourselves. We are at liberty to say to him: 'Nevertheless I am continually *with thee.*'

At this point your question will surely be: But how can we accomplish this? Let me hasten to answer that *we* cannot do this. Yet there is something much more excellent than what we can do. Here it is written: *Thou dost hold my right hand.*

Therefore, I hold on because *you* hold me. I am continually because you are with me. I say 'nevertheless' because you say 'nevertheless' to me who is unable to say so in his own strength and undeserving of your assurance. You say 'nevertheless' to me who is what he is, has done what he has done and does what he does, who is perhaps a doubter, a man of little faith, if not an atheist. Because you hold me, I say: 'Nevertheless I am continually with thee.' I say so because evidently my sorrow is not my own, but yours; because you have taken my sorrow and the sorrow of all mankind to your heart, have borne them in your life and vindicated them in your death on the cross; because 'in soul and body, whether I live or die, I am not my own, but I belong unto my most faithful Lord and Saviour Jesus Christ'.

You hold me, and therefore I am bold to say: *Nevertheless I am continually with thee.*

One more thing remains to be considered. The text states: *Thou dost hold my right hand.* The right hand is man's strong and skilful hand (provided he is not left-handed). It is the hand to work, to write and, if necessary, to fight with. We give the right hand of fellowship when we greet one another. The right hand symbolizes ourselves, indeed ourselves where it counts, where we mean business, where our heart is. We are not asked to extend the right hand of fellowship to the Lord God. There is no need for it whatever. The gesture is belated. *He* holds us by our right hand, he takes us seriously where it counts to be taken seriously. This is our situation. I shall never forget how one of my sons, long since grown up to be a missionary in Indonesia, asked me as a little boy: 'Do you know who Mr Essential is?' 'No, who is he?' 'He is the heavenly Father.' God proves himself as Mr Essential by letting us be essential in his sight, by holding our right hand with his right hand. We are not even asked where to put our right hand. Impossible to hold on to him in a non-essential, off-handed way. Our right hand is no longer free. He holds it! It is already in his own hand!

Let me conclude with a question. Who are you? Who am I? The answer is: one whom God holds by his right hand, on whose heart and lips God has laid the confession of faithfulness and the great comfort: *Nevertheless I am continually with thee.* Glory be to the Father, and to the Son, and to the Holy Ghost. Amen.

O Lord, our God! This is thy unspeakable glory that we may call out for thee 'O Lord, our God, our Creator, our Saviour'—that thou knowest and lovest us all and desirest to be known and loved by each one of us—that thou seest and governest all our ways—that we all come from thee and go to thee.

We spread out everything before thee—our cares, that thou wouldst care for them—our anxiety, that thou wouldst still it—our hopes and desires, that thy will be done and not our own—our sins, that thou wouldst forgive them—our thoughts and longings, that thou wouldst purify them—our whole life in this our time, that thou wouldst lead it to the resurrection of the body and the life everlasting.

We remember before thee all the inmates of this house and all the other captives around the world. Be thou with our loved ones at home, with all the poor, the sick, the distressed and the afflicted. Enlighten the thoughts and govern the actions of all those in our land and in all other lands who are responsible for justice and order and peace. Let the day break through Jesus Christ, our Lord, in whose name we pray: 'Our Father . . .'

UNTO YOU IS BORN THIS DAY
A SAVIOUR

Christmas 1954

Dear heavenly Father! As we are gathered here to rejoice in thy dear Son who became man and a brother for our sake, we beseech thee most heartily—show us how great is the mercy, loving-kindness and help that thou hast prepared in him for us all!

Open our hearts and our understanding and we shall grasp that in him is forgiveness of all our sins, is seed and growth for a new life, is comfort and counsel in life and death, is hope for the whole world!

Create in us a true spirit of freedom to go out humbly and courageously, and meet thy Son who comes to us!

Grant today to the whole Christian Church and to the world as well that many may break through the glitter and vanity of the holiday season and truly celebrate Christmas with us. Amen.

MY DEAR BROTHERS AND SISTERS, now we have heard the Christmas story. We heard about Caesar Augustus and the governor of Syria, about Joseph and Mary and the birth of the baby in Bethlehem, about the shepherds in the fields and the appearance of the angel of the Lord in their midst, about the multitude of the heavenly host, praising God and saying *Glory to God in the highest, and on earth peace among men with whom he is pleased!*

I surely would like to know what went on in your minds when you heard this story! Perhaps two or three among you did not listen very carefully—this happens quite often—and the story passed over their heads like a cloud or a puff of smoke. Should I read the story again for the benefit of these people of wandering thoughts? It is worth repeating twice, even a hundred times! But for today we shall leave it at this.

Or perhaps there are those, men or women, who thought I was telling a nice fairy tale, far removed from the realities of life? Too beautiful to be true? What shall I tell them? Shall I debate with them? I shall gladly do so at any other time. But presently ours is a more important task.

Perhaps also some among you, when they heard the story, were reminded of the days of their youth long since gone-by. They thought of Sunday School where they were told this story for the first time, of the Christmas tree, of the presents and the candies, of how beautiful things were, but are no longer and never will be again. What shall I answer? Shall I put on a serious face and say: Forget about Christmas trees and Christmas sentiments and concentrate on the Christmas story itself? This will not be my reply either.

I only intended to show you, my dear friends, that *these* are our human reactions to the Christmas story, which truly is the story of us all. It is much more important, more true and more real than all the stories in history books and novels and all the broadcast and printed news put together! A little absentminded-ness, a little unbelief and a little Christmas sentiment, these are our reactions, not only yours, but mine as well!

Until the *angel of the Lord* appears and shakes us up! The angel of the Lord most certainly passed this night through the streets and the homes and the squares of Basel. He was here for those who celebrated Christmas Eve in loneliness and distress, or on the contrary in fun and frivolity. He is here for all those who are still asleep and maybe have something to sleep off. He is passing through the churches of our town this morning. How does he tell the good news to all these people? How do they listen to him or do not listen at all? However, let us not refer to other people, but rather focus on ourselves. The angel of the Lord most certainly is here in our midst to speak and to be heard. It only remains for me to make you aware of his presence and attentive to his words, so that together we may listen, and ponder what he has to say.

An angel! That is—a *messenger*, who has some news for us. You might quite simply think of the mailman bringing you some news. The angel of the Lord is God's messenger carrying the news of the Christmas story. You see, if *he* announces the news, absent-mindedness, unbelief and lofty sentiments are swept away, for the angel of the Lord descends directly from God to us. I recently saw a picture where he precipitates straight from heaven to earth, almost like lightning. Granted, this is an image, and yet it is real. If the angel of the Lord is the carrier of the news, the lightning strikes and illumines the truth: the glory of the Lord shone around them and the night was as light as the day. As a Christmas hymn has it: 'Eternal light from heaven descends, the earth all new and bright extends, and vanquished is the darkest night, we all may be children of light.'

And now let us try to hear and understand part of what the

angel of the Lord told the shepherds and tells us now. *For to you is born this day in the city of David a Saviour!* These words *you—this day—a Saviour* contain the whole Christmas story. We shall meditate on each one of them.

'*To you* is born this day a Saviour', says the angel of the Lord. This is already tremendously important.

First, the news of the birth of the child in Bethlehem is quite different from the news, let's say, of the arrival of the Emperor of Ethiopia in our country. You may have heard about this event. We were flattered that the emperor liked our country and that his hosts were equally impressed with their guest. But we hear this news—don't we?—thinking: 'Why should I be concerned? This is entirely a matter between him and them.' In contrast, the angel of the Lord points to Bethlehem, saying, 'for *to you* is born this day a Saviour'. For your sake God was not content to be God but willed to become man; for you he emptied himself that you may be exalted; for you he gave himself that you may be lifted up and drawn unto him. The wondrous deed brought him no gain, fulfilled no need of his. It was accomplished only for you, for us. The Christmas story then is a story that is enacted with us and for us.

The news of the birth of the child in Bethlehem is not to be likened to a statement made in a textbook. The angel of the Lord was no professor as I am. A professor would perhaps have said: 'To mankind is born a Saviour.' So what? We are apt to deduce that mankind in general does not include me, is only meant for others. It is like in a movie or a play where we are confronted with people who are not ourselves. In contrast, the angel of the Lord points to the shepherds and points to *us*. His news is directly addressed to us: '*To you* is born this day a Saviour!' You, regardless of who you are, whether or not you understand the message, whether or not you are good and pious people. The news is meant for you. For your benefit the

Christmas story happened. Again, it does not take place without us; we are involved in it.

The news of the birth of the child in Bethlehem affects us differently than the morning mail. When the mailman arrives, we eagerly ask: 'Anything for me?' And seizing the letter, we withdraw to read it. We resent intruders peeping over our shoulder and want to read the letter alone, since this is a private matter. In contrast, the event of Bethlehem is no private matter. '*To you* is born this day a Saviour.' True, the angel of the Lord points to you and to me, individually, yet he addresses us corporately. His news ties us together like brothers and sisters who share a wonderful present from their father. No one is first, no one is last, no one gets preference, no one gets short-changed, and most important, not a single one goes wanting. He who was born in Bethlehem is the eldest brother of us all. Therefore we pray in his name '*Our* Father'. Therefore we do not pray, 'Give me this day my daily bread', but rather, 'Give us this day *our* daily bread'. And forgive *us* our trespasses! And lead *us* not into temptation, but deliver *us* from evil!' Therefore also we go to the Lord's Supper as to the table of the Lord, and eat from *one* bread and drink from *one* cup. 'Take and eat! Drink ye all!' Therefore the Christian life is one great communion, a fellowship with the Saviour and hence a fellowship among brothers. Where there is no communion with the Saviour, there is no communion among brothers, and where there is no communion among brothers, there is no communion with the Saviour. The one is not possible without the other. This is the content of the angel's call '*to you*', and we should keep it in mind.

'To you—*this day* is born a Saviour,' says the angel of the Lord. When Christ was born it was *this day*! A new day dawned in the middle of the night. Christ himself was and is the sun of this day and of everyday. The new day is not only Christmas Day, it is the day of our life. *This day* refers not only to the *past*, to 'once upon a time'.

Far from it. The angel of the Lord today announces the same news he then announced to the shepherds. We live in the new day which God has made. We hear of a possible new beginning in our human relations and conditions, in the history of our lives and even in the history of the world. We are told that yesterday's misery, guilt and fear, though still existing, have been mercifully covered and no longer harm us, because to us is born a Saviour. We may take courage, pull ourselves together and venture a new start. Human experience does not warrant such confidence, yet this is the assurance of the angel of the Lord. Because the Saviour is born, therefore a new day has dawned!

This day implies *not only tomorrow*. Certainly *also tomorrow*! He who was born on that first Christmas Day will not die ever again but lives and reigns eternally. Yet we ought not to dwell on the morrow. You know well enough the kind of people that love to repeat: *Morgen, morgen, nur nicht heute!* (German proverb, in translation: Tomorrow, tomorrow, but never today!) 'Let's wait and see' is a dangerous saying. Who knows if we shall be around tomorrow? Surely the Saviour will be there, but what about us? Who knows whether we shall hear the good news once again tomorrow and shall be free to respond? The decision is not in our hands. Only yesterday I came across a word of our Swiss writer Jeremias Gotthelf: 'Life is not a light; a light can be kindled again: life is a fire given by God to burn on earth just once and never more.' My dear friends, let us pay heed lest we miss the hour of this fire right here and now. We are told elsewhere: 'O that today you would hearken to his voice! Harden not your hearts!'

This is what the angel of the Lord has to tell us when he announces '*this day*'! And now we hear: 'To you this day is born *a Saviour*'! This is the very heart of the Christmas story. To you this day is born *a Saviour*. Of the many thoughts that come to mind here, I shall choose just one.

What does the word *Saviour* convey? The Saviour is he who brings us *salvation*, granting us all things needed and salutary. He is the helper, the liberator, the redeemer as no man, but God alone, can be and really is; he stands by us, he rescues us, he delivers us from the deadly plague. Now we live because he, the *Saviour*, is with us.

The Saviour is also he who has wrought salvation *free of charge*, without our deserving and without our assistance, and without our paying the bill. All we are asked to do is to stretch out our hands, to receive the gift, and to be thankful.

The Saviour is he who brings salvation to *all*, without reservation or exception, simply because we all need him and because he is the Son of God who is the Father of us all. When he was made man, he became the brother of us all. *To you this day is born a Saviour*, says the angel of the Lord.

This, then, is the Christmas story. You see, we cannot possibly hear this story and not look away from ourselves, from our own life with its cares and burdens. There he is, our great God and Saviour, and here we are, human beings, and now it is true that he is for me, is for us. Impossible to hear his story without hearing our own. It is the great *transformation* that has been worked in us once and for all, the great *joy* it has released in us, and the great *calling* we have received to set out on the way he shows us.

What shall we do now? Shall we continue in our old ways, in absentmindedness, in disbelief, perhaps in some lofty Christian sentiments? Or shall we awake and rise, set out on our journey and turn about? The angel of the Lord does not compel anybody. Even less can I compel! A forced listening to the Christmas story, a forced participation in the story, is of no avail. We must willingly listen, and willingly participate.

And suddenly there was with the angel a multitude of the heavenly host praising God and saying, 'Glory to God in the highest, and on earth peace among men with whom he is well pleased.' Our place is not among the angels; we live here on earth, in this city, in this house. Yet when we hear about this song of praise and when we realize that God did not send one angel alone, but that the multitude of the heavenly host was present with their song of praise, might we not be carried away just as we fall in step when a good band plays or unconsciously hum or whistle a well-known tune that falls on our ears? That would be it! Then we would freely listen to and freely participate in the Christmas story. Amen.

O Lord, our God! Thou art great, exalted and holy above us and above all men. This is thy glory that thou dost not forget us, not abandon us, not reject us despite all that speaks against us. In thy dear Son Jesus Christ, our Lord, thou hast given us nothing less than thyself and all that is thine. We praise thee that we are invited as guests at the table of thy mercy throughout our life and beyond.

We spread before thee all that troubles us, our mistakes, our errors and our transgressions, our sorrows and cares, also our rebellion and our bitterness—our whole heart, our whole life, better known to thee than it is to ourselves. We commit all this into the faithful hands which thou hast outstretched in our Saviour. Take us as we are; strengthen us when we are weak; grant us, the poor, the bounties of thy blessings, FOR THE SAKE OF JX OUR LORD. IN HIS NAME WE PRAY, AMEN

Let thy lovingkindness shine upon our loved ones, upon all prisoners, and those in the pangs of misery, illness or death. Bestow upon the judges the spirit of justice and upon the rulers of this world some measure of thy wisdom, that they may strive for peace on earth. Give a clear and courageous witness to all who are called to preach thy word here and abroad.

Gathering up all our concerns we call on thee as our Saviour has permitted and commanded us to do: 'Our Father . . .'

YOU WILL LIVE ALSO

Easter Sunday 1955

O Lord, our God! Here we are, celebrating Easter together in thy presence. This is the day when thou hast revealed thy beloved Son, our Lord Jesus Christ, to be the living Saviour. He has taken upon himself all our sins, our human misery and death and in our place expiated, suffered and, once for all, conquered and dismissed them.

We know well our plight and thou knowest it even better. Yet now we approach thee with thanksgiving for the freedom we have to look away from ourselves and to thee who hast wrought this mighty work for the world and for us also.

Grant sincerity to our speaking and our listening—that thy true word may govern, move and replenish us in this hour—that it may comfort, encourage and admonish us all by its power—that our poor praise may be pleasing to thee!

Let this come to pass among us and everywhere in town and country, nearby and afar, wherever people are gathered today to hear and to grasp thy promise of resurrection and life! Shed thy mercy upon thy people! Amen.

MY DEAR BROTHERS AND SISTERS, *I live*. Jesus Christ has said that, and now he is saying to us again: 'I live.'

Let me recall another of his sayings which may help to explain these two short words. 'Where two or three are gathered in my name, there I am in the midst of them.' We are gathered here in his name, and hence not in our own. Not because we enjoy dealing with him, but because he is pleased to deal with us. Not because we are for him, but because he is for us. Not because we have earned the right of his companionship, but because he has paid the highest price for our companionship with him. He sealed it when he came into the world, calling out: 'Come to me, all who labour and are heavy-laden, and I will give you rest.' Not only did he express this invitation and promise in words; he validated it through the mighty act of his entire life and death. Through this call and this act he has created a fellowship on earth, where at all times and in all places he is the Lord, the shepherd and the teacher. He has gathered us into his fold right here and now. Because this is so, he is in our midst even here and now, testifying to the truth: 'I live.' He is not in the tomb; he is risen, as we have heard it read from the Gospel. He himself tells us to forget about everything else and to stick firmly to this fact: 'I live.'

Clearly, if he says 'I live', he says something more, something else and better than if I, or one of you for that matter, said it. What indeed is our life compared to his? True, our life is at stake. It is significant that the affirmation 'I live' is immediately followed by another 'and you will live also'. Hence when Jesus says 'I live', he speaks about the redemption of our life, of its freedom and holiness, its righteousness and glory. Yet if we are to understand the affirmation about ourselves, we first must be attentive to the all-inclusive affirmation about him. 'I live'—a life very different from yours, not at all to be compared with it.

I live. As Jesus Christ's own statement this means: 'I live as true man *my divine life.*' We must take this quite seriously and literally. I live the life of the eternal and almighty God who has created heaven and earth and is the source and fullness of life. What does this mean? Perhaps that I live this divine life of abundance intent on laying hold on it, keeping it and enjoying it for myself, as a rich man likes to lay hold on his possessions, keep them and enjoy them? Or that I offer it as a most peculiar and most precious treasure for your admiration at a distance? Or maybe that I hand out occasional alms from its bounty? No, my brothers and sisters, this is not the life of God, not the life of him who, in time and eternity, refuses to be for himself and by himself but wills to be and is *our* God, sharing with us all the riches of his life.

I live. When spoken by Jesus this means: 'I live my divine life *for you.* I live it fully by loving you. Without you I do not care to be the Son of God or to enjoy my divine life. I live it fully by pouring it out. Without reticence or reservation I give it away for you. I live my divine life by taking your place, the place that is allotted to you. I become what you are (not just some of you, but all of you), a prisoner, a convict, sentenced to death. This I do, by the power of my divine life spent for you, that the darkness and perplexity, the sorrow, anxiety and despair, the sin and guilt of your petty, wicked and miserable life may be cancelled out, and your own death may once and for all be extinguished and annihilated. In this giving of myself, in this saving power I live my life, my divine life.'

I live. Asserted by Jesus Christ this means: 'I live *my human life* as the true Son of God. It is indeed the life of a weak, of a solitary, of a tempted man dying in shame, like you, totally like you. How so? Perhaps I reserve the better part for myself after all? Or perhaps I rebel against my human existence in misery, or try hard to put up with it in mute and fierce defiance? No, definitely not so. In so doing I would not really want to be like you, your neighbour, your brother, the neighbour and brother of the most needy. I would desert and betray you. I would refuse to be the one who lives from God's mercy alone. I would deny my sincere desire to be true man, let alone to be God's child.'

I live. This affirmation by Jesus means: 'I live my human life without opposition or resistance *as your own*, such as life is. I live it in acceptance of the fact that all folly and wickedness, all anxiety and despair, your own and that of the world, are laid upon my shoulders. I live it by carrying this burden in obedience to God who has laid it upon me, and thereby I lift it from you. I convert, renew and baptize in my person your human life in all its aspects, transforming your perdition into redemption, your sin into righteousness, your death into life. This I do so that you may be born again in me to new beings who, in hope, give God glory and stop seeking their own. This I do so that you may grow in me into men with whom God is well pleased. Lifting it up for your sake, I live my life, my human life, my life as your own.'

Therefore: '*I live* only to pour out my divine life in your service and to lift up my human life in the service of God.' This is the Christ who appeared to his followers on Easter morning. This is the Christ who is in our midst here and now, proclaiming: 'I live.' The subsequent affirmation concerning ourselves is contained in this primary affirmation by Jesus about himself.

You will live also. In our German Bibles this statement reads: 'And you shall live also.' Yet the significant fact to remember is precisely not an obligation we are invited or urged to fulfil, so that we may, or may not, live. We are not merely given a chance; nor is an offer made to us. 'You will live also' is a promise. It is an announcement referring to the future, to our future. 'You will live also' succeeds the present of, and our presence in, the 'I live' like two succeeds one, B succeeds A, the thunder succeeds the lightning. He who comprehends the 'I live' will right away comprehend the 'You will live also'. You are a people whose future issues from my life and hence does not lie in your sin and guilt, but in true righteousness and holiness. Not in sadness, but in joy, not in captivity, but in freedom, not in death, but in life. From your present participation in my life, you may anticipate *this* and no other future.

Let me explain further what is at stake for us when we have heard both, 'I live' and, immediately following, 'You will live also'.

It is now all-important for us to cling to this truth that *he*, Jesus Christ, in *his* life, is our present. Not our past is our present. Not the great darkness casting its shadows out of yesterday into today. Not what we rightly or wrongly hold against ourselves and probably against others as well. Not the world with its accusations and we with our counter-accusations. Not even the well-deserved divine wrath against us, let alone our grumbling against God, or our secret thought that there might be no God after all. Therefore, not we ourselves, as we are today or think we are, make up our present. He, Jesus Christ, his life is our present: his divine life poured out for us, and his human life, our life, lifted up in him. This is what counts. This is what is true and valid. From this point on we may continue our journey into the future. And this is the future which grows out of this present: *You will live also*.

It is now all-important for us to accept his gifts for the journey, to be equipped and nourished by him. My brothers and sisters, none of us can help himself, can create life from within himself, or acquire anything by himself. Whatever man wishes to seize bears the mark of sin and death. But there is really no need for us to seize anything. We may simply receive what is already laid out for us. Everything is prepared for us all. Whatever had been in disorder has been put to order. We only need to accept the

already established order. We only need to see what is spread out before our eyes and to hear what is said with unmistakable clarity. We only need to open and stretch out our hands instead of ever again hiding them in our pockets and clenching our fists. We only need to open our mouth and eat and drink, instead of setting our teeth, as we used to do when we were children. We only need to walk forward instead of going backwards in the manner of fools.

It is vitally important for us to let grow the tiny root of confidence, of earnestness, of joy, which seeks ground in our hearts and minds, in our thoughts and intentions and opinions— perhaps this very Easter morning. It is truly impossible that Jesus Christ proclaims: 'I live', without the answer arising from somewhere within us: 'Yes, you live, and because you live, I shall live also, I may and I can and I want to live! I for whom you, true God, became a true man—I for whom you died and rose again—I for whom you accomplished all and everything needed in time and eternity!'

It is all-important now that not one among us consider himself excluded, either too great or too insignificant or too godless. It is all important that each one of us consider himself included, a partaker of God's mercy in the life of our Lord as revealed in his resurrection from the dead on Easter morning. It is all-important that we believe humbly yet courageously that we are those born again in him to a living hope: *You will live also*.

I am at the end. We are privileged now to approach the Lord's table. The Lord's Supper is quite simply the sign of what we have said: Jesus Christ is in our midst, he, the man in whom God himself has poured out his life for our sake and in whom our life is lifted up to God. Holy Communion is the sign that Jesus Christ is our beginning and we may rise up and walk into the future where we shall live. The Lord himself gives us strength, food and drink for our journey, from *one* bread and from *one* cup, because he is One, he the One for us all. My dear brothers

and sisters, I do not want to oppress or compel any one among you when I add: Shall we not all here present go to the Lord's table together? Holy Communion is offered to all, as surely as the living Jesus Christ himself is for all, as surely as all of us are not divided in him, but belong together as brothers and sisters, all of us poor sinners, all of us rich through his mercy. Amen.

O Lord, our God, our Father in Jesus Christ thy Son, our brother! We give thee thanks that everything is as we have attempted to say and to hear it once more today. We are sorry to have so often been blind and deaf to the light and the meaning of thy word. We are sorry for all the perversion of our life, resulting from this obstinacy. We know very well that without thee we go astray, time and again. We ask thee for thy Holy Spirit to touch us, to awaken us, to make us attentive, humble and courageous.

This we ask not only each one for himself, but each one for all others, for the inmates of this house and all prisoners throughout the world, for the sick in body and soul, for the destitute and the refugees, for all those whose grief and needs are hidden from us, though not from thee. We ask this also for our families, for all parents, teachers and children, for Government and court officials, for the preachers and missionaries of thy gospel.

Help them and help us all to bear what must be borne, but also to think, to speak and to do what is right, above all to believe, to love and to hope according to the measure thou wilt give to them and to us.

'Our Father . . .'

SAVED BY GRACE

14 August 1955

O Lord, our God! Through thy Son, our Lord Jesus Christ, thou hast made us thy children. We have heard thy voice and have gathered here to give thee praise, to listen to thy word, to call upon thee and to entrust to thy care our burdens and our needs. Be thou in our midst and be our teacher—that all anxiety and despair, all vanity and defiance within us, all our unbelief and superstition may diminish and thy greatness and goodness may show forth;

—that our hearts may be open to one another, that we may understand each other, and help one another;

—that this hour may be an hour of light wherein we may catch sight of the open sky and thus of the dawn on this dark earth.

The old has passed away, behold, the new has come. This is true, and it is true for us, as certainly as thou art in Jesus Christ the Saviour of us all. But only thou canst truly tell us and show us that this is so. Speak and show then the truth to us and to all those who pray with us this Sunday morning. They pray for us. And we are praying for them. Grant their requests and ours! Amen.

My dear brothers and sisters, I now read a passage from the Letter of the Apostle Paul to the Ephesians (2.5): *By grace have you been saved*. This, I think, is brief enough for it to be remembered by all, for it to impress itself upon you and, if it be God's will, to be understood.

We are gathered here this Sunday morning to hear this word: *By grace you have been saved!* Whatever else we do, praying and singing, is but an answer to this word spoken to us by God himself. The prophets and apostles wrote a strange book, called the Bible, for the very purpose of testifying to this fact before mankind. The Bible alone contains this sentence. We do not read it in Kant or in Schopenhauer, or in any book of natural or secular history, and certainly not in any novel, but in the Bible alone. In order to hear this word we need what is called the Church—the company of Christians, of human beings called and willing to listen together to the Bible and through it to the word of God. This is the word of God: *By grace you have been saved!*

Someone once said to me: 'I need not go to church. I need not read the Bible. I know already what the Church teaches and what the Bible says: "Do what is right and fear no one!" ' Let me say this at this point: If this were the message at stake, I would most certainly not have come here. My time is too precious and so is yours. To say that, neither prophets nor apostles, neither Bible, Jesus Christ nor God are needed. Anybody is at liberty to say this to himself. By the same token this saying is void of any new, of any very special and exciting message. It does not help anyone. I have never seen a smile on the face of a person reassuring himself with this kind of talk. As a rule, those who use it are a sad-looking lot, revealing all too easily that this word does not help them, does not comfort them, does not bring them joy.

Let us hear therefore what the Bible says and what we as Christians are called to hear together: *By grace you have been saved!* No man can say this to himself. Neither can he say it to someone else. This can only be said by God to each one of us.

It takes Jesus Christ to make this saying true. It takes the apostles to communicate it. And our gathering here as Christians is needed to spread it among us. This is why it is truly news, and very special news, the most exciting news of all, the most helpful thing also, indeed the only helpful thing.

'By grace *you* have been saved!' How strange to have this message addressed to us! Who are we, anyway? Let me tell you quite frankly: we are all together great sinners. Please understand me: I include myself. I stand ready to confess being the greatest sinner among you all; yet you may then not exclude yourself from the group! Sinners are people who in the judgment of God, and perhaps of their own consciences, missed and lost their way, who are not just a little, but totally guilty, hopelessly indebted and lost not only in time, but in eternity. We are such sinners. And we are prisoners. Believe me, there is a captivity much worse than the captivity in this house. There are walls much thicker and doors much heavier than those closed upon you. All of us, the people without and you within, are prisoners of our own obstinacy, of our many greeds, of our various anxieties, of our mistrust and in the last analysis of our unbelief. We are all sufferers. Most of all we suffer from ourselves. We each make life difficult for ourselves and in so doing for our fellowmen. We suffer from life's lack of meaning. We suffer in the shadow of death and of eternal judgment toward which we are moving. We spend our life in the midst of a whole world of sin and captivity and suffering.

But now listen. Into the depth of our predicament the word is spoken from on high: *By grace you have been saved!* To be saved does not just mean to be a little encouraged, a little comforted, a little relieved. It means to be pulled out like a log from a burning fire. You have been saved! We are not told: you may be saved sometimes, or a little bit. No, you *have been* saved, totally and for all times. You? Yes, we! Not just any other people, more pious and better than we are, no, we, each one of us.

This is so because Jesus Christ is our brother and, through his life and death, has become our Saviour who has wrought our salvation. He is the word of God for us. And this word is: *By grace you have been saved!*

You probably all know the legend of the rider who crossed the frozen Lake of Constance by night without knowing it. When he reached the opposite shore and was told whence he came, he broke down, horrified. This is the human situation when the sky opens and the earth is bright, when we may hear: *By grace you have been saved!* In such a moment we are like that terrified rider. When we hear this word we involuntarily look back, do we not, asking ourselves: Where have I been? Over an abyss, in mortal danger! What did I do? The most foolish thing I ever attempted! What happened? I was doomed and miraculously escaped and now I am safe! You ask: 'Do we really live in such danger?' Yes, we live on the brink of death. But we have been saved. Look at our Saviour and at our salvation! Look at Jesus Christ on the cross, accused, sentenced and punished instead of us! Do you know for whose sake he is hanging there? For *our* sake—because of *our* sin—sharing *our* captivity—burdened with *our* suffering! He nails *our* life to the cross. This is how God had to deal with *us*. From this darkness he has saved *us*. He who is not shattered after hearing this news may not yet have grasped the word of God: *By grace you have been saved!*

But more important than the fear of sudden death is the knowledge of life imparted to us: 'By grace you have been *saved*!' Therefore, we have reached the shore, the Lake of Constance is behind us, we may breathe freely, even though we still are in the grip of panic, and rightly so. This panic is but an aftermath. By virtue of the good news the sky truly opens and the earth is bright. What a glorious relief to be told that there I was, in that darkness, over that abyss, on the brink of death, but there I am no longer. Through this folly I lived, but I cannot and I will not do it again, never again. This happened, but it must not and it will not happen again. My sin, my captivity, my suffering are yesterday's reality, not today's. They are things of my past, not of the present nor of the future. I have been *saved*! Is this really so, is this the truth? Look once again to Jesus Christ in his death upon the cross. Look and try to understand that what he did and suffered he did and suffered for you, for me, for us all. He carried our sin, our captivity and our suffering, and did not carry it in vain. *He carried it away*. He acted as the captain of us all. He broke through the ranks of our enemies. He has already won the battle, our battle. All we have to do is to follow him, to be victorious with him. Through him, in him we are saved. Our sin has no longer any power over us. Our prison door is open. Our suffering has come to an end. This is a great word indeed. The word of God *is* indeed a great word. And we would deny him, we would deny the Lord Jesus Christ, were we to deny the greatness of this word: He sets us free. When he, the Son of God, sets us free, we are *truly* free.

Because we are saved by no other than Jesus Christ, we are saved *by grace*. This means that we did not deserve to be saved. What we deserved would be quite different. We cannot secure salvation for ourselves. Did you read in the newspapers the other day that man will soon be able to produce an artificial moon? But we cannot produce our salvation. No one can be proud of being saved. Each one can only fold his hands in great lowliness of heart and be thankful like a child. Consequently we shall never possess salvation as our property. We may only receive it as a gift over and over again, with hands outstretched. '*By grace* you have been saved!' This means constantly to look away from ourselves to God and to the man on the cross where this truth is revealed. This truth is ever anew to be believed and to be grasped by faith. To believe means to look to Jesus Christ and to God and to trust that there is the truth for us, for our lives, for the life of all men.

Is it not a pity that we rebel against this very truth in the depth of our hearts? Indeed, we dislike hearing that we are saved by grace, and by grace alone. We do not appreciate that God does not owe us anything, that we are bound to live from his goodness alone, that we are left with nothing but the great humility, the thankfulness of a child presented with many gifts. For we do not like at all to look away from ourselves. We would much prefer to withdraw into our own inner circle, not unlike the snail into its shell, and to be with ourselves. To put it bluntly: we do not like to believe. And yet grace and therefore faith as I just described it is the beginning of the true life of freedom, of a carefree heart, of joy deep within, of love of God and neighbour, of great and assured hope! And yet grace and faith would make things so very simple in our lives!

Dear brothers and sisters, where do we stand now? One thing is certain: the bright day *has dawned*, the sun of God *does shine* into our dark lives, even though we may close our eyes to its radiance. His voice *does call* us from heaven, even though we may obstruct our ears. The bread of life *is offered* to us, even though we are inclined to clench our fists instead of opening our hands to take the bread and eat it. The door of our prison *is open*, even though, strangely enough, we prefer to remain within. God has put the house in order, even though we like to mess it up all over again. *By grace you have been saved!*—this is true, even though we may not believe it, may not accept it as valid for ourselves and unfortunately in so doing may forego its benefits. *Why* should we want to forego the benefits? *Why* should we not want to believe? *Why* do we not go out through the open door? *Why* do we not open our clenched fists? *Why* do we obstruct our ears? *Why* are we blindfolded? Honestly, *why?*

One remark in reply must suffice. All this is so because perhaps we failed to pray fervently enough for a change within ourselves, on our part. That God is God, not only almighty, but merciful and good, that he wills and does what is best for us, that Jesus Christ died for us to set us free, that by grace, in him, we have been saved—all this need *not* be a concern of our prayers. All these things are true apart from our own deeds and prayers. But to believe, to accept, to let it be true for us, to begin to live with this truth, to believe it not only with our minds and with our lips, but also with our hearts and with all our life, so that our fellowmen may sense it, and finally to let our total existence be immersed in the great divine truth, *by grace you have been saved*, this is to be the concern of our prayers. No human being has ever prayed for this in vain. If anyone asks for this, the answer is already being given and faith begins. And because no one has ever asked for this in vain, no one may omit praying like a little child for the assurance that God's truth, this terrible, this glorious truth, is shining even today, a small, yet increasingly bright light. *By grace you have been saved*. Ask that you may believe this and it will be given you; seek this, and you will find it; knock on this door, and it will be opened to you.

This, my dear friends, is what I have been privileged and empowered to tell you of the good news as the word of God today. Amen.

O Lord, our God! Thou seest and hearest us. Thou knowest each one of us far better than we know ourselves. Thou lovest us without our deserving it. Thou hast helped us and dost help us still, although we are ever again inclined to spoil thy work by wanting to help ourselves. Thou art the Judge, but thou art also the Saviour of the poor and per-plexed human race. For this we give thee thanks. For this we praise thee. We rejoice in the prospect of seeing with our own eyes on thy great day what we already now may believe if thou makest us free to do so.

Make us free to believe! Give us the true, honest and active faith in thee and in thy truth! Give it to many! Give it to all men! Give it to the peoples and their governments, to the rich and to the poor, to the healthy and to the sick, to the prisoners and to those who think they are free, to the old and to the young, to the joyful and to the sorrowful, to the heavy-laden and to the light-minded! There is no one who does not stand in need of faith, no one to whom the promise of faith is denied. Tell all our people, ourselves included, that thou art their merciful God and Father and ours! This we ask thee in the name of Jesus Christ who commanded us to pray: 'Our Father . . .'

LOOK UP TO HIM!

Ascension Day 1956

O Lord our God! Our father through thy Son who became our
brother!

*Thou callest us: 'Return, you sons of man! Lift up your hearts!
Seek what is above!' With these words thou hast summoned us this
very morning. Here we are, each one with his life which is not his
own, but wholly thine, wholly in thy hands; each one with his sins,
great and small, which only thou canst forgive; each one with his
sorrows which only thou canst transform into joy. Here we are nevertheless each one also with his own secret hope that thou wilt prove
to be his almighty and merciful God.*

*We all know that only one thing will please and honour thee—
earnest asking for thy Spirit, earnest searching for thy truth, earnest
longing for thy help and guidance. We also know that even these can
only be thy work in us. Wake us up, O Lord, that we may be awake!*

*Grant that everything we do in this hour be according to thy will,
when we pray and sing, when we speak and listen, when we partake
of the Lord's Supper. Grant this request to all that join us today in
celebrating the Ascension of our Lord Jesus Christ, even the bedridden
in the hospitals, the mentally disturbed of our local institution, the
countless crowd of those unaware that they themselves are prisoners,
are sick or disturbed, and perhaps have never heard of thee as their
comfort, their hope and their redeemer. Shed thy light upon them and
upon us, through Jesus Christ, our Lord. Amen.*

Look up to him, your face will shine, and you shall never be ashamed.

MY DEAR BROTHERS AND SISTERS, '*Look up to him!*' This is what we commemorate on Ascension Day: the urgent invitation, the permission and the command, the freedom we enjoy as Christians and the obedience that is expected from us to look up to him, to Jesus Christ, who lived for us, died and rose again. He is our Saviour who watches over us like an older brother watches over his younger brothers and sisters, yet in his protection is also their example and their master.

He is above, in *heaven*. We are below, on earth. When we hear the word 'heaven' we are inclined to think of the great blue or grey sphere arching over us with its sunshine, its clouds and its rain, or of the even higher world of the stars. This is what we may have in mind right now. In the vocabulary of the Bible, however, this 'heaven' is nothing but the sign of an even higher reality. There is a realm *above and beyond* the world of man, which is lost to our sight, to our understanding, to our penetration, and even more to our dominion. It is way above and beyond us. In biblical language heaven is the dwelling place, the throne, of God. It is the mystery encompassing us everywhere. *There* Jesus Christ lives. He is in the centre of this mystery beyond. Of all men, he alone went there, all by himself, in order to be there and from there, from the throne of God, the Lord and Saviour of us all. Therefore: *Look up to him!*

To 'look up' alone would not do. 'Chin up!' we are wont to say to a friend in distress. You may have heard this 'chin up!' yourself. But this is somewhat of a problem. Could it not be that above and beyond us, in heaven, we are confronted with a stark and merciless mirror, reflecting our own human affliction? We might see once more the wrong done to us by our neighbours and the wrong done by us to them, but now magnified and projected into the infinite. We might see our guilt, our inner

anxieties and our outward affliction, all we call fate, and finally
death itself. All these could be included in the mystery beyond,
in heaven! This heaven would lie like a dark cloud over our
heads, or like one of those dungeons where they used to keep
prisoners in centuries gone-by, or even like a coffin lid, burying
us alive under its weight. Does anyone wish to look up there?
No, we'd better forget about such a menace from above! But
what is the use of trying not to think of it if it is nevertheless real?
Things could even be much worse. God himself could be like
this heaven: a Holy Being, rightfully turned against us, a
sinister tyrant, the very enemy of mankind, or perhaps
simply an indifferent God who willed for unknown reasons
to set us under this cloud, under this dungeon, under this
coffin lid. Many of us, even all of us in our desperate
moments and years, hold on to this mental picture of heaven and
of God. No, 'look up' by itself would be no help at all.

But to look up to him, to Jesus Christ—this is our help! He is
over us. He is in the centre of that encompassing mystery. He
is in heaven. Who is Jesus Christ? He is the man in whom God
has not only expressed his love, not only painted it on the wall,
but put it to work. He is the principal actor who has taken upon
himself and has overcome our human affliction, the injustice
done by ourselves and by everybody else, our guilt and anxiety,
our fate, even our death. These evils no longer threaten us from
above. They are below us, even under our feet. He is the Son of
God, who was made man in our likeness, who became our
brother, in order that we may be with him children of the
Father, that we may all be reunited with God and may share in
his blessings: in his severe kindness and in his kind severity, and
lastly in the eternal life for which we are meant and which is
meant for us. This Jesus Christ, this mighty man, this Son of God
is in heaven. And so is God. In the face of the Son the face of the
heavenly Father is made to shine.

'Look up *to him*!' This means: Let him be who he is, above us,

in heaven. Acknowledge and believe that he is up there and lives
for us! Keep firmly in mind that he intervenes with all his
power in your behalf, but keep firmly in mind also that you
belong to him and not to yourselves. Say very simply 'yes'. Say
that he is right and wants to make things right for you, indeed
has already made them right for us all. Is this an exaggerated
claim? Has he really made things right for all of us? Even for
the most miserable, the most afflicted and the most embittered
of human beings? Yes! Even for the most grievous offenders?
Yes! Even for the godless—or those pretending to be godless,
as may be the case with some of your fellow-prisoners who
declined to be with us this morning? Yes! Jesus Christ has made
things right for them and for us all. He is willing to do it time
and again. To look up to Jesus Christ means to accept his
righteousness and to be content; not to question any more that
he is right. This is the message of the Ascension: we are invited
to look up to him, to this Jesus Christ, or, to use a more familiar
expression, to believe in him.

'Look up to him *and your face will shine!*' What an announcement! What a promise and assurance! People, very ordinary
human beings, with illumined faces! Not angels in heaven, but
men and women on earth! Not some lucky inhabitants of a
beautiful island far away, but people here in Basel, here in this
house! Not some very special people among us, but each and
every one of us! Might this be the true meaning of the promise?
Yes, this is the true meaning. But is this the only real meaning?
Yes, this is the only real meaning. Look up to him, and your face
will shine!

When a man, any one of us, obeys this imperative and looks
up to him, to Jesus Christ, a momentous change takes place in
him. The greatest revolution is unimportant by comparison.
The transformation cannot be overlooked. It is manifest, quite
simply, in so much as he who looks up to him and believes in

him, here on earth, here in Basel, here in this house, may become a child of God. It is an inward change, yet it cannot possibly remain hidden. As soon as it occurs, it presses forcefully for outward manifestation. A great and enduring light brightly dawns on such a person. This light is reflected on his face, in his eyes, in his behaviour, in his words and deeds. Such a person experiences joy in the midst of his sorrows and sufferings, much as he still may sigh and grumble. Not a cheap and superficial joy that passes, but deep-seated, lasting joy. It transforms man in his sadness into a fundamentally joyful being. We may as well admit it: he has got something to laugh at, and he just cannot help laughing, even though he does not feel like it. His laughter is not bad, but good, not a mockery, but an open and relaxing laughter, not a diplomatic gesture as has recently become so fashionable in politics, but honest and sincere laughter, coming from the bottom of man's heart. Such light and joy and laughter are ours when we look up to him, to Jesus Christ. He is the one who makes us radiant. We ourselves cannot put on bright faces. But neither can we prevent them from shining. Looking up to him, our faces shine.

Dear brothers and sisters, why is it then that our faces are not bright? If they were, we would feel fine, would be glad to live uprightly and contentedly in spite of adversities, wouldn't we? Just because we would feel fine, we would be radiant. But something more important has to be considered here. If the light, the joy and the laughter of God's children really pressed for outward manifestation and became visible, our fellowmen around us would notice it in the first place. Don't you agree with me that such a change would make a quite definite impact on them? It would be a sign that there are different and far better things in store than they are wont to see. It would give them confidence, courage and hope. They would be relieved, as we have been relieved this last week by the sun after a long winter. Why relieved? Because such a bright face would be the reflection of heaven on earth, of Jesus Christ, of God the Father himself. What a relief that light would be for them and for us! Do we not all together long for its appearance?

We should get the simple truth straight, dear friends. We are in the world not to comfort ourselves, but to comfort others. Yet the one and only genuine comfort we may offer to our fellowmen is this reflection of heaven, of Jesus Christ, of God himself, as it appears on a radiant face. Why don't we do it? Why do we withhold from them the one comfort of mutual benefit? Why are the faces we show each other at best superior looking, serious, questioning, sorrowful and reproachful faces, at worst even grimaces or lifeless masks, real Carnival masks? Why don't our faces shine?

Let me say only one thing here. It could easily be otherwise. We could greet each other with bright faces! We could comfort each other. We, here, today! Where the Spirit of the Lord is, there is freedom for man to comfort his neighbour. 'He who believes in me,' says Jesus Christ himself in another Scripture passage, 'out of his heart shall flow rivers of living water.' This happens when we look up to him. No one has ever looked up to him without this miracle happening. No one who gets slowly used to looking up to him has failed to glimpse light around him. The dark earth on which we live has always become bright whenever man looked up to him, and believed in him.

'Look up to him, your face will shine, *and you shall never be ashamed.*' I just mentioned the 'dark' earth. Reading the newspapers, looking around at the world and into our own hearts and lives, we can't possibly deny that the earth is really dark, that we live in a world to be afraid in. Why afraid? Because we all live under the threat of being put to shame, and rightly so. This would not only imply that we have blundered here and there, but that our whole life, with all our thoughts, desires and accomplishments, might be in truth, in God's judgment and verdict, a failure, an infamy, a total loss. This is the great threat. This is why the ground shakes under our feet, the sky is covered with clouds, and the earth, so beautifully created, darkens. Indeed we should be put to shame.

But now we hear the very opposite. 'You shall never be ashamed.' What I would like to do, dear brothers and sisters, is to ask you, each and all, to get up together and like a choir repeat: 'We must never be ashamed!' Each one would have to repeat it for himself and lastly I would repeat it for myself: 'I must never be ashamed!' This is what counts. We shall not be, I shall not be ashamed, not when looking up to him. Not because we deserve to be spared the shame! Not even because our faces shine when raised to him. Our radiance will be and must be a sign that we will not be put to shame. It is an evidence of the relationship established between God and ourselves. And this is the power of the relationship: what is true and valid in heaven, what Jesus Christ has done for us, what has been accomplished by him, man's redemption, justification and preservation, is true and valid on earth also. The Father does not put us, his children, to shame when we look up to Jesus. In consequence we, his children, may never be ashamed. This we may know, this may be out strength, this may be our life, if only we look up to him, fearlessly and brightly. May each one repeat in his heart: 'Bless the Lord, O my soul; and all that is within me, bless his holy name! Bless the Lord, O my soul, and forget not all his benefits; who forgives all your iniquity, who heals all your diseases, who redeems your life from the pit, who crowns you with steadfast love and mercy.' With these words let us go to the Lord's Supper. Amen.

O Lord, our God! We are grateful that all is as we have tried to say with our weak words and to hear with our weak ears. Our praise of thy name will never cease, because thy mercy and truth are without end, and are always greater and more glorious than we may ever express or grasp.

Bring about the first fruits of thy spirit in our hearts and lives, and in all we shall think and say and do today and tomorrow! Grant us to be faithful stewards of thy gifts, making good use of the time which thou hast given to work for its fulfilment, for thy glory and our salvation!

Continue to have mercy on us and on all men, on our families, on all the suffering and tempted, on the authorities of this town and country, on civil servants, teachers and students, on the judges, the accused and the sentenced, on the pastors and their congregations, on the missionaries and those to whom they are privileged to proclaim thy truth, on the Evangelicals in Spain and in South America and on their misguided oppressors. Where thou dost not build through thy word, Church and world are built in vain. Let thy word run its course and reach many. Let it go to all men with the power to shine, to heal and to win which it has whenever it is rightly preached and received in the power of thy Holy Spirit.

'Our Father . . .'

MY HOPE IS IN THEE

5 August 1956

O Lord, our God! Here we are met because this is the day which we call Sunday. Sunday in remembrance of the sun of righteousness that thou hast made to rise for all men in the resurrection of thy dear Son Jesus Christ. Sunday in anticipation of the last day when all men shall see this sun, shall fear thee and rejoice in thee.

None of us has any claim to appear worthy before thee, not one of us. We know and thou knowest even better how far we departed from thy ways in all we have been, thought, said and done up to this hour.

We are together before thee only because thou hast descended into our human world of darkness and art willing to enter in our midst right now. Only because thou dost call us thy people and accept our unworthy praise in the lovingkindness and power of thy word and spirit.

Give us for our common tasks, we pray, the humility and the joy of people who cannot but be grateful! Give humility and joy also to all others gathered today before thee in this city and elsewhere. Through Jesus Christ, our Lord, in whose name we call on thee: 'Our Father . . .'

And now, Lord, what comfort shall I seek? My hope is in thee.

DEAR BROTHERS AND SISTERS, it is a tremendous thing that we are invited right now to take this affirmation on our lips, to repeat it and to join in the chorus, '*My hope is in thee.*'

Hope is joy, is expectation of a hidden treasure in store for us. Although invisible at present, it will most certainly be uncovered one day, and will be ours. To hope is to live in this expectation and in this joy.

But our text specifies, '*My hope is in thee*', in God. The hope in God is the one totally genuine and totally reliable hope. *Genuine* because God is not just *a* treasure and blessing, but *the* blessing. He is the source of all good things; they overflow from his goodness. *Reliable* because God is faithful. He will not deceive us; nor will he let us await for ever his self-disclosure. It is a tremendous thing, not at all self-evident, that we may say and repeat: '*My hope is in thee.*'

None of you shall now think and say, 'Well, once upon a time this may have been said in the Bible, probably by some good, pious and presumably happy person. But for this very reason it is not meant for me, and I cannot make it my own. I am not such a good, pious, let alone a happy person.'

No such thoughts, no such talk, dear friends! Granted, the people who speak in the Bible, including the man who affirms in the 39th Psalm: '*My hope is in thee!*' were rather peculiar people; but peculiar only because God encountered them and dealt with them in his own way. Most certainly not peculiar because of their particular characteristics or talents that might have distinguished them from their fellowmen. As God dealt with them in his peculiar way, they were peculiarly exposed to the human predicament, much more so than others. Listen to the passage immediately preceding our text: 'Behold, thou hast made my days a few handbreadths and my lifetime is as nothing

in thy sight. Surely every man stands as a mere breath! Surely
man goes about as a shadow! Surely for nought are they in
turmoil; man heaps up, and knows not who will gather!' You
see, it is from this situation—we might also say into this situation
—that the people of the Bible affirm: 'My hope is in thee.'
They call us to repeat it for ourselves and to repeat it with them:
'My hope is in thee.'

Above all, don't think and say of me who happens to preach
this Sunday sermon: 'Well, what idle talk! He did no wrong
that brought him before the judge. He has no prison term to
serve. He may walk freely wherever he likes and, what is more,
he is a professor of theology and as such presumably a convinced
Christian if not a half-saint. What idle thought and talk is this,
"My hope is in thee"?'

Once more, none of this! Do you know what a convinced
Christian is? A convinced Christian is one who knows a little
better than others do that we all, without exception, have done
so much wrong that we are to appear before the judge not once,
but throughout our life. And mind you, he is the highest ranking
and most severe judge there is, and we shall have to expiate for
what we have been, thought, said and done. A convinced
Christian knows precisely that in reality no one walks freely
wherever he likes! Let me read another passage from the same
39th Psalm: 'When thou dost chasten man with rebukes for sin,
thou dost consume like a moth what is dear to him; surely every
man is a mere breath!' Surely every man—this is what a convinced Christian knows. Only then and on this ground he may
and he even must confess 'My hope is in thee', he may and he
must bear witness to others that they are equally free to hope in
God.

Let us now consider the question which precedes the affirmation of hope: 'What shall be my comfort?'

If someone seeks comfort, he is likely to seek and to find ways and means to ease and to relieve the great and small anxieties, troubles and fears of his life, just as we give a patient an injection —or he gives one to himself. The illness, it is true, will not be cured, but at least the pain will be alleviated for a while and the illness banished from his thoughts. Some injections give a temporary feeling of strength and health to the patient. Likewise there are means of comfort that convey to the user the impression of extraordinary well-being.

However, comfort is not the equivalent of hope in God. Rather, we seek comfort as long as we fail to realize that we may hope in God. To seek comfort is a substitute, and to live by such comfort is to live a bogus life, a life on false assumptions. It proves to be a merely superficial, preliminary, and temporary relief, no better than the effect of those injections which never eliminate the roots of the disease and only kill the pain for a short while. The anxieties, troubles and fears of life remain—and so do their consequences.

Thus all comfort-seeking is overshadowed by the question, 'What kind of comfort shall I seek?', or 'What is the use of comfort?' I need more than comfort. I need help, I need redemption. But as long as we fail to realize that we may hope in God, we shall go around in circles, constantly trying to seek comfort, constantly discovering that comfort does not help, does not even comfort in the long run! Let me give a few illustrations.

As you well know, we can comfort ourselves with a cigarette, or with a newspaper, or by turning on the radio, or with a little liquor. Why not? This is called 'diversion'. There are even nobler diversions like music, work, reading, perhaps reading that involves a great deal of work. Well, diversions are all right, but you know the result. In the end we are back where we were, in our old misery. What comfort shall I seek?

Or we can also seek comfort by comparing ourselves with others. John Doe is no better off than I am, indeed he is no better than myself. Yet ultimately I can only live as I am as an individual, with my heart and my emotions, my suffering and my destiny, and with my conscience. What is the use of comparing? What comfort shall I seek?

We can certainly try to seek comfort in ourselves. All of us do it at times. If all are against me, I will be for myself. I will confide in my own strength and be content. Do you know the story of the Negro who had the habit of speaking aloud to himself? When he was asked to explain his odd behaviour, he answered, 'For one thing, I like to talk to an intelligent person; for another, I like to be addressed by an intelligent one.' Or have you heard that other story about the man who believed in the one and only true Church which had but one member for the time being—he himself?

Marvellous, isn't it? But is it really so marvellous, so wonderful, to take refuge in ourselves, to trust only ourselves? If so, we have to assume that we are pleased and satisfied with ourselves. For a short run and for a while we may imagine that we are. But beware! Somewhere along the way the most dreadful doubt ever to befall a man will raise its head. It is the doubt of oneself. Again we are thrown back to the question, 'What comfort shall I seek?'

But why not take comfort from the thought of a dear fellow human being, a man or a woman, a companion or a friend, a trustworthy person whom we may expect to act as a good Samaritan? Very well, this is good comfort. Finding such a person might even be the very best comfort. If we are lucky enough to find one! But even when we do find one he will be but one more comfort. For even the dearest and best person, the best Samaritan, remains a human being. He cannot shoulder my responsibility. He has his own limitations. He may fail. And he may be taken from me. There is no getting away from it, a moment comes in our life when no one can take our place, when we are utterly left to ourselves. 'What comfort shall I seek?'

Do you know the real reason why all our attempts to comfort ourselves must finally collapse, like cardhouses we may build but not inhabit? Even though we do not lack the means of comfort and even though they and our comforting arguments are not negligible? Indeed are we not compelled to admit that they have their value? Why then do they disappoint us?

Let me tell you, dear friends, that there is not a bad, but a good, even the very best reason for this disappointment. It is quite simply that God is *God, our* God, who does not abandon us in spite of our abandoning him ever and again; who is present and at work in our lives; who tells us, whether we are attentive to his voice or not, 'In me there is not only comfort, but hope. I am your helper and redeemer.' Not only does God forbid us to comfort ourselves; he prevents us from doing so. He will not rest until we acknowledge who and what he is for us, until we realize that we may hope in him. Therefore, for this very reason our various consolatory arguments dissolve like bubbles!

'*Lord*, what shall be my comfort?' Thus asks the writer of the psalm. Don't be content to sigh 'what shall be my comfort?' Add the small word 'Lord' and you will be on the right path. Because you confront me, therefore no other comfort is sufficient; therefore all other comforts flee; therefore I am compelled to inquire again and again what my comfort shall be; therefore I cannot find the answer to this question. Because you, my great and good Lord, are present and invite me to hope in you.

And now let us follow this line of thought. Let us speak not about God, but to him, the ever present Lord. Let us say: 'My life is bound up with you: as the Lord of heaven and earth and the Lord of all men you are also my Lord and God. I am bound up with you: not because I am willing and able to face you—we are all unwilling and unable to do so—but because from all eternity you willed to be bound up with me, and truly are. Because my life is not in my own hands, but in yours, whether

I know you or not, whether I honour you or not, whether I love you or not. Because without my doing you are also my King and Judge. Because you are my justification, my peace, my joy, my salvation, although I do not deserve and cannot deserve it. Because your son has become my brother, and because as the brother of your son, our Lord Jesus Christ, I may be your child! In his entire life and death your son and our brother has mightily yearned for you and joyfully confessed his hope in you. Declining to seek comfort and consolation he relied on you, he trusted you, he obeyed you in the thick of the discomfort and desolation of human life, our life. Thus he proved to be your son. Thus he also acted as our brother. For he was obedient not as an individual, not for his own sake, but in the place of us all. In behalf of all humanity, in our behalf, he turned to you and sealed his existence with the great word "I hope in you".'

I think we understand by now that it will not help to put our heads together and debate how we can engineer this hope by our own efforts. What we do on our own strength is doomed. Hope in God cannot be engineered; it can only be enacted. It is enacted when we accept as valid for you and me the great 'I hope in you' spoken by Jesus Christ for us, when we subscribe, so to speak, to this word, when we sign it very humbly, and approve it, however hesitantly.

Believe me, our feeble voice will become strong in this confession; it will pierce the sky, call God to our side, and provide strength to live. Believe furthermore that God gives each one of us the freedom to approve and to sign our names under the word that Jesus Christ has spoken and still speaks for us. If we make good use of this freedom, our bogus life patched up with our various comforts will be replaced by true life. We shall receive eyes that will perceive light in the deepest darkness, feet to stand on firm ground regardless of our insecurity, busy hands although we are tired, and joyous hearts that triumph over the dreariness and despair of our existence. The hidden God himself holds us and sustains us even now, when we do not yet see him. In him *we hope*.

One last word. You ask perhaps 'what about comfort? Do we not need it and may we not have it?' The answer is: 'Don't worry; only one thing will be impossible with him who, as a brother of Jesus Christ, hopes in God: the desire or attempt to comfort himself.' We can do without it. When we hope in God we *are* comforted, and believe me, the big and small pleasures we were talking about earlier will be ours. We may work; we may listen to music; we may read books; we may perhaps also find a dear friend and good Samaritan who comes to our rescue; we may even gain and keep some measure of self-confidence. Many things may then have their rightful place, but there will be none to which we may cling, none whereby we may comfort ourselves. What we are unable to provide for ourselves will be given to us, not as the main gift, but as a secondary one—as a bonus, so to speak, to encourage us to hope in God; as a token of his goodness, a parable of his compassion. I might also say as the rays of the one and only comfort which is not mere comfort, but is the sun of righteousness, of redemption, of life eternal. It is the comfort to belong with body and soul, both in life and in death, not to myself but to my faithful Saviour, Jesus Christ. Amen.

Dear heavenly Father! We implore thee to give thy Holy Spirit to us all now and evermore, that he may awaken us, enlighten us, encourage and enable us to dare the small and yet so important leap from the comforts of our own choosing to hope in thee. Draw us away from ourselves unto thee! Forbid that we hide from thy face or try to do so! Show us how glorious thou art and how glorious it is to trust in thee and to obey thee!

We ask this gift for all mankind. Let the people and their rulers bow to thy word that they be bent on justice and peace on earth. Let thy truth be proclaimed by word and by deed to all the sick, the prisoners, the afflicted, the oppressed, the unbelievers. Let them hear thy truth, comprehend it and take it to heart as the answer to their sighing and crying. Lead the Christians of all Churches and confessions to a fresh discovery of thy word and a new faithfulness in its service. Make thy truth shine here and now in our human tangles and wrangles until at last it illumines forever all and everything.

Glory be to thee who in Jesus Christ, thy Son, makes us free to confess—and to abide in this confession—'we hope in thee,' Amen.

YOU SHALL BE MY PEOPLE

7 October 1956[1]

O Lord, our God! Thou knowest who we are: human beings with a good or with a bad conscience, some content and others discontent, some secure and others insecure, convinced Christians and nominal Christians, believers, half-believers and unbelievers.

Thou also knowest whence we have come: from the bonds of family and friendship or from great loneliness, from peaceful prosperity or from manifold adversities and troubles, from happy, tense or broken homes, from the core of the Christian community or from its fringe.

Here we are gathered now in thy presence: in all our diversity equally unrighteous before thee and before each other, equally subject to death, equally lost without thy mercy, yet also equally sharing the promise and the gift of thy grace offered to all in thy dear Son, our Lord Jesus Christ.

We have come together to praise and glorify thee as we let thee speak to us. We pray that this may come to pass in this evening hour when Sunday is far spent and daily work lies ahead. In the name of thy Son, our Lord, and with his words we call on thee: 'Our Father . . .'

1 Sermon in the Bruderholzkapelle, Basel.

I will walk among you, and will be your God, and you shall be my people.
LEVITICUS 26.12

DEAR FRIENDS, DEAR BROTHERS AND SISTERS, thus said the Lord to his people Israel according to the Old Testament: '*I will walk among you, and will be your God, and you shall be my people.*' A great deal could be said about the meaning of this assurance for the people of Israel up to this day. There can be no doubt that the history of Israel reached its climax in Jesus Christ, an offspring of Israel. The promise of our text was also fulfilled in him. It thereby became a trumpet sound that rings around the earth. It rings for us also, even especially for us. I shall try briefly to explain it.

First we are told, *I will walk among you.* To walk is to advance in a definite direction, to move about from one place to another, like the milkman or the postman or the gasman goes to and fro the streets of the town, from one house to the next. The verb is most commonly used in the Bible to describe the conduct of people. It may then be said that their 'ways' are pleasing or unpleasing, straight or crooked in God's sight. Strangely enough, the verb occasionally even refers to God's own moving about. Right in the beginning of the Bible we read that the Lord God was walking in the Garden in the cool of the day. And now we hear him saying, 'I will walk among you'. We learn that God is not motionless. He is no inflexible being. He is not the prisoner of his own eternity. No, God is on his way; God comes and goes; God is the principal actor of a drama. God *walks*: he is the *living* God.

'I will walk *among you.*' The roads where God walks and moves about as the living God are our roads, where we walk, drive our cars and board our street-cars, where we go our own ways. He walks through our houses with their living rooms and dining rooms and kitchens and bedrooms, through our gardens, our places of work and of amusement, and certainly also through our church buildings. Why not also through this chapel here on the hill? God is not absent; he is not elsewhere. He lives in heaven, but he lives also on earth, even in our neighbourhood, among us and with us. He is the God who always and everywhere is *near*.

'I will walk among you' is sometimes translated as 'I will walk *in your midst*'. This is more precise. The living God is the centre, the source and the origin, but also the destination of our restless existence. The history of our lives unfolds because in their innermost centre God's own history unfolds. We are the work of his hands. He walks among us, in our midst. We are but the circle of which he is the centre. This binds us to him, this binds together the fragments of our lives, this binds us to one another. Therefore, God is not at the periphery. Neither is he the boundary, as some philosophers like to maintain today. True, our piety and our faith possibly occupy but the periphery of our lives, while the vital centre lies elsewhere. The presence of a Reformed Church in Basel is apt to be a phenomenon of only marginal interest to those who converse in the taverns or write and read the newspapers. But we are concerned at this point neither with our piety, nor even with the Church, but with God himself. He is not at the periphery. He is closer to us than we are to ourselves. He knows us better than we know ourselves. He gives us a fairer deal than we ourselves, even with the best will and knowledge in the world, can provide. Hence his ways involve us all. In all the disparity of man and human situations, he is the *one* God, now here and now there, for you and for me.

Because he is the *living* God, who is near and who is one, he really walks among us, in our midst, whether we take notice or not, whether we like it or not. He walks among the old and the young, among the sick and the healthy, among the extroverts and the introverts, among the good and the evil. Because he is God *almighty*, he never grows weary. And let no one imagine he might succeed in delaying or hindering God! Because he is the *holy* God, he cannot be deceived. He cannot be snubbed as we are likely to snub other people, nor can he be mastered as we think we master certain people or opinions and situations, if not our destiny itself. And because he is the *merciful* God, he will not take offence. He will not grow bitter, nor will he be confounded in his love.

> Like a father from his children
> Never takes his love away,
> Though they often turn against him
> And deceive him day by day,
> Even my most grievous failure
> Does my faithful Lord forgive,
> Chastening me with wrath and mercy,
> Not the sword, that I may live.

This, then, is how the holy God, walking in our midst, deals with us, whether we work or rest, whether we are glad or sad, whether we wake or sleep—in this year of 1956 and certainly also in the years thereafter—in time and even more in eternity when we shall see him face to face, the living God who is near and who is one.

I go on to the second promise of our text. *And will be your God.* God says to us: 'Since I am the living God who is near and who is one, almighty, holy and merciful, I will be *your* God. I will care for you. I will carry you in my eternal thoughts. I will love you, but also call you to obedience in my service where I can make good use of you. With *you* I am speaking this very moment.'

God says furthermore: 'As the creator of heaven and earth, as Lord of all men, as eternal king and victor who has the first word and the last, I will belong to you, and you may call me "Our *Father*! Our God!" Each one for himself may call me "My Father! My God!" For you I gave myself in my Son. For you I will be your God, for you as you are, ridden with anxiety, worries and frustration, for your sins and for your death, but also for your resurrection from the dead, for your life in time and eternity.'

God continues: 'I will stand by you, I will take sides with you,

I will declare my unconditional solidarity with you, against all odds, against the whole world and all of mankind if need be, in particular against your own self!' Is it not true that man is his own worst enemy? Is not the most valuable partisan and helper one who, just because he is for us, dares to be mightily against us? God is this strong *partisan and helper*. We might also say: God in his divine determination and his divine perfection will say 'yes' to us. But God's 'yes' is a holy and wholesome 'yes', comprising always a 'no'. It is the 'no' to everything in us and about us which he must reject for his sake and our own. He treats us like a doctor who prescribes pills and medication we utterly dislike. I shall never forget how as a little boy I had to drink a glass of cod-liver oil every morning for many years. It tasted terrible, but it obviously did me some good. The doctor may even send us to the hospital, certainly not a very cheerful place. He may perform a minor or major operation, a most disagreable undertaking indeed, yet how important for recovery! This is how God's 'yes' with the loathsome 'no' in it, works. Be not anxious. God says 'yes' to us fully, unconditionally and unquestionably. He wills, he is able, to rescue us, to support us, to put us on our feet, to make us free and joyful. This is what 'I will be your God' means. In short, I will be what is beneficial to you, your good against all evil, your protection against all disaster, your peace against all strife. In this way, walking among you, I will be your God!

And now the third and last promise. *And you shall be my people.* 'As I will walk among you, as I will be your God, you shall be *my people.*' This is perhaps the most inconceivable and most exalting affirmation, precisely because it concerns us so directly. 'You —my people!' For this much we know—don't we? In no way can we ever presume to be his, God's people. Nor can we ever merit or acquire this status through our own efforts. Yet this we are told, this we may hear and believe—that we shall be his people.

'*You*, really *you* shall be my people!' Such as you are now, not as future saints or angels. You with your transitory life and work that one day will come to its end in the cemetery. You with your restless thoughts, fluttering in all directions like excited hens. You with your inappropriate words, for ever incapable of expressing what you really mean and what should be said. You with your big and small lies, with your subtle or sharp cruelties, with your slackness and sometimes with your shabby tricks, with your excitements and depressions. You the dying who are utterly lost without me. *You*, you shall be my people!'

'*My* people' implies that you shall be those who find in me their Lord and Judge, yet at the same time their merciful Father. You shall fear me, love me, call on me, turn to me every morning anew, seeking my face. Even better, you shall be my witnesses before the others who do not know me, who cannot know me, who refuse to know me. You shall be the light of the world! You, living with me, under my wing and as my servants, you shall be *my* people.

'My *people*' is not to be overlooked either. You are not a sandpile of individuals, one here in his house and there another on his balcony; one here with his wife and there another with his children; a money-seeker here and a fun-seeker there. Not as these scattered individuals, but called and gathered by me, you shall be a people of brothers and sisters. You shall support and help one another, perhaps timidly, perhaps boldly. You shall witness to one another, with or without words, that I live and walk among you, I, your God, in the midst of you, my *people*!

Is it not truly the most inconceivable and the most exalting message we have heard this evening that we are to be God's people? I am glad I did not invent it, and hence it is not my responsibility to defend it. My only task and privilege is to tell you that God himself said so and says so until this day. On his authority I may and I must say to you, 'Yes, you shall be my people!' Let us hear this assurance as well as the two preceding ones as God's word. Let us take it to heart, let us take it home, and maybe ponder it a while before we fall asleep tonight. 'I will walk among you! I will be your God! You shall be my people!'

I am at the end. I tried to explain this Bible passage as the word of God fulfilled in Jesus Christ. Read and heard, understood and believed in this light, this word radiates infinite power. It then not only says, 'I will walk among you', but 'I *walk* among you!' Not only 'I will be your God', but 'I *am* your God!' Not only 'You shall be my people', but 'You *are* my people!' Do you sense the power of this word? The power of him in whom it is fulfilled and becomes a present reality? Be it as it may, because this is the word of God fulfilled in Jesus Christ, you and I may be assured beyond disquiet or doubt that things stand exactly as I have tried to tell you today. Amen.

O Lord, our shepherd! We give thanks for thy word, eternally new, valid and powerful! We are sorry that we so often do not understand it or misunderstand it, dumb or wanton as we are. Keep thy word for us, we beseech thee, and keep us steadfast in thy word. We live by its power. Without its light we would lose the ground under our feet. We depend on thy speaking with us again and again. We trust that thou wilt do it as thou hast done in the past.

Relying on thee we shall now lie down to rest and take up again our work in the morning. Relying on thee we include in our prayer all our fellowmen in the neighbourhood, in this town and country, and all over the world. Thou art their God as well. Hasten to show thyself as their God! In particular to the needy, the sick and the mentally ill, to the prisoners, the sorrow-stricken and the wayward; also to those who bear heavy responsibilities in the service of society, in public administration, economic affairs, in education and in law; also to the ministers of this congregation and of all congregations here and elsewhere.

Lord, have mercy upon us! Thou hast done so abundantly. Why should we doubt? Thou wilt again do so abundantly. Amen.

THE GOSPEL OF GOD

23 December 1956

O Lord, thou leadest us again this year to the light, the joy and the festivity of Christmas, the day when thy love is manifest in the greatest event of all. For thou so loved the world that thou gavest thine only begotten Son that whosoever believeth in him shall not perish, but have everlasting life.

What gift may we bring to thee? There is so much darkness in our human relationships and in our own hearts! So much confused thinking, so much coldness and resistance, so much folly and hatred! So many things which are displeasing in thy sight and separate us from each other, which are of no help to us! So much that is directly opposed to the glad tidings of Christmas!

What canst thou do with these our gifts? What with such people as we all are? And yet it is nothing else than these miserable gifts, together with ourselves, that thou expectest at Christmas. Thou wilt lift the burden from us and give us Jesus our Saviour instead, and with him a new heaven and a new earth, new hearts and a new mind, new clarity and new hope for us and all mankind.

Be with us as we prepare ourselves on this last Sunday in Advent to receive him as thy gift! Grant that we speak and listen and pray rightly, in truly grateful wonder at what thou didst plan, what thou hast already decided and done for all of us.

'Our Father . . .'

Jesus came into Galilee, preaching the gospel of God, and saying: The time is fulfilled, and the kingdom at hand; repent, and believe in the gospel.

MARK 1.14-15

DEAR BROTHERS AND SISTERS, *Jesus came into Galilee.* The Galilee into which he came was a region where the Jews, mingling with the Gentiles, had in many ways adjusted to Gentile customs and thereby lost their good name. Into this Galilee, and to these people, *Jesus came.* It is the very-same region where the Jews who call themselves Israelis today live in bitter strife with their Arab neighbours. Jesus came there almost two thousand years ago and he comes there today. We are now in the present. Jesus comes also to Suez and to Port Said where the old European powers and the awakening peoples of Africa and Asia clash. He comes into Hungary where a whole nation fights for its freedom, desperately and yet not in despair. He comes also into Warsaw, into Prague, into Moscow, where the unity, firmness and security of a system believed indestructible has begun to crack. Yes, Jesus comes also into Switzerland, into Basel, where so much money has been collected and so much good done for the Hungarians during the past few weeks, but where at the same time people have been remarkably content to hurl abuses at the nasty Communists far away, as if this were of much help to anyone. Even more important, Jesus comes to us too; he comes into this prison house, he comes to all its inmates, governors and wardens. That he comes to all of us is the event of Christmas. Yes, he comes to all and everyone. If he is not welcome, he is nevertheless present as a silent guest and listener, and as a silent yet impartial judge as well. Above all he is *here*, as the hidden Saviour of each and every one of us, fulfilling all human need. For he is the Lord to whom all power is given on earth as in heaven. That he comes to us all is the event of Christmas.

Who was he and who is he, this Jesus? Let us not search afar. The text which we read gives a very simple and yet a very clear answer. He was and he is the one who *preaches the gospel of God*. A preacher is one who speaks up loudly, who even shouts, like the oldtime towncrier. Jesus was and is such a towncrier. His message is the gospel, the good news, the glad tidings, a message which defies all derision and puts an end to all sadness. It is this 'gospel of God' which Jesus preaches. This is a very strange and beautiful expression. It says very clearly that Jesus proclaiming the good news is in the service not of man, but of God, acting not of his own will, but by the will of the Father. *The gospel of God* means furthermore that the good news does not contain any instruction about how the world fares or should fare. It is neither a bird's eye view of the world, nor a platform for the world. It is the good news of what God is, wants and does, and is, wants and does for us. Jesus' coming as the bearer of this gospel of God is the event of Christmas. Because he came and he comes we all sang even as little children: 'O come all ye faithful, joyful and triumphant!' This is why we light the Christmas tree today. This is why we prepare big and small presents. This is why every human being, even the most downcast, may lift his head at Christmas. Should we not know a little more about this gospel of God? Infinitely rich as this gospel is, we shall follow today the invitation of our text to dwell on the essentials.

First: *The time is fulfilled, and the kingdom of God is at hand.* We must hear this news in the same way as we hear the news of the daily headlines. This is a *message*. Something has happened, a fact is established, so far ignored by us, claiming our immediate attention.

Second: *Repent, and believe in the gospel!* We must hear this in the same way as we hear a call to arms. This is a *command*. Act now, immediately, according to the impact made on you by the message.

I shall try to give a short explanation of both the message and the command.

The time is fulfilled and the kingdom is at hand. Both sentences belong together and, as a whole, comprise the message which we are asked to take to heart. The time is fulfilled because the kingdom of God is at hand. And the kingdom of God being at hand, the time is fulfilled.

The time is fulfilled. The hour has struck, not the quarter hour, not the half hour, not the three-quarter hour, but the full hour has struck. The many seconds and minutes have all had their time, have all moved toward this one climax. Now it has come and the clock strikes. The old hour is past, a new one has begun. For the kingdom of God is at hand. Christmas comes, and is here! Truly, every nation has had its time: the English with their Empire, the French with their great nation, Hitler with his 'Reich of a thousand years', the Americans with their eagerness to buy the whole world, the Russians with their world Communism, the Hungarians with their proud and heroic spirit, and also the Swiss with their great self-sufficiency and self-righteousness. They all have had their time. The hour strikes, the old is past, a new hour has begun. The kingdom of God is at hand! Christmas is here!

Let me put this message in different words. In your life and in mine everything had its time. We have had good and bad days, dreamed good and bad dreams, had high hopes and bitter disappointments, had our glorious as well as our darkest moments. Everything has gone its course up to this very moment. But now the hour strikes, the old is past, the new begins. The kingdom of God is at hand! It is Christmas! Why? What event took place? What does this mean, *the kingdom of God is at hand*? A kingdom is a dominion one not only has but exercises. The kingdom of God is the dominion exercised by him. *The kingdom is at hand*, it has descended from heaven to earth, from eternity into time. Now, here and today God shows forth his power. God himself has come to us, and has taken the lead from our hands into his own because we had failed in our individual and corporate affairs. He will not only take the reins—he has *already* done so. This is *the kingdom of God* at *hand*. He who loves us infinitely more than we love ourselves saw the misery in which we engulf ourselves by thinking we know how to love and understand ourselves. He saw the hardships, the atrocities, the injustice and the disorder, he saw our false securities and our breakdowns. He could not stand it any more. He could not bear any longer being God on high without being God on earth, our helper, saviour and redeemer. And he not only wanted action, he *took* it! This is his kingdom at hand. He has called us, the unworthy, he has led us to his house and opened the door for us, he even gave us our own key, he has invited us to his table and given us of his bread and of his wine. He has acted like a true Father for us. He has given us a home with himself where we may live and work, and even play and rejoice as his children—a home from which we shall not be driven out. We shall never more be strangers, or- phans, refugees. This is what he has done. This is how his kingdom is *at hand*.

This, therefore, is Christmas. This is the fulfilment of time! The crucial hour has struck! This is the *message* brought by Jesus when he proclaims the gospel of God.

There is also the call to arms, *the command*. The tone has changed. We are ordered to *repent and believe in the gospel*. Again the two sentences belong together. Repent by believing in the gospel! Believe in the gospel by repenting—there is no other true repentance.

You see that now, and only now, it is our turn. Only now! Without the preceding message this command is null and void. How could we repent and believe without the kingdom of God at hand? But the message has been announced by Jesus. Now the preaching of the gospel of God reaches our hearts, our conscience, our thoughts, and our lives. There is no other real response to the message but to repent and to believe, now, here, today and without delay, and this response may, indeed must, be given.

What may, indeed what must, take place? *Repent!* The term 'repent' is likely to evoke in us something like remorse, shame and

contrition. And rightly so. To repent certainly means to make
an aboutface, to leave behind many, if not all, things which we
assumed were necessary, important, or exciting, and to start
afresh in a new direction. Because *the kingdom of God is at hand*
many things have become outdated and hence useless. Contrition and shame are certainly in order. This does not alter,
however, the basic fact that repentance as decreed by the gospel
of God is a joyful venture. He who repents might well put on
his very best clothes. For where is the beginning of repentance
except in rejoicing over the kingdom that is at hand? Repentance
is not a dark moment, it is a bright moment. It is the passage
from an ugly bygone hour into God's bright new hour. To
repent is to come back home to the place which God prepared
for us. It means to enter into God's house which God opened
for us, to sit down and to eat at the table prepared by the Father,
to breathe freely, to live at long last. We have not yet lived at
all—but now we may live! It is both a command and a gift
that we repent, not because we must, but because we may.

How do we go about repenting? We are told to *believe in the
gospel.* I wonder what comes to your mind when you think of
believing. Maybe what you once heard in confirmation class?
Or what you hear from your chaplain or just now from me?
Indeed it might be well to believe again very firmly what you
once learned and what your chaplain tells you, even to believe me
a little right now! But there is a much more decisive acceptance
at stake. *Believe in the gospel!* we are told. To believe in the
gospel is to accept the good news told not by man, but by God,
to accept it as told by God, to make it our own, to let it take root
in our hearts and grow and bring forth fruit. This leads quite
naturally to repentance. An even simpler expression for belief
in the gospel is gratitude. Yes, dear friends, to be a little truly
thankful for this good news, for what it says to you and to me
and to all mankind! To believe most certainly includes gratitude
for not being left alone. Whenever we believe, we are made

part of a community. I do not refer to any association, not even to any particular congregation, but to the communion of all those who are allowed to believe together.

And to believe in the gospel in the deepest sense means, quite simply, *to stand by the messenger who brought us the gospel of God, to stand by Jesus Christ.* The hour that strikes is his hour. It is the hour of his coming, of his advent, of his birth, and thereby the hour of Christmas. What is the kingdom of God save himself —the Son of the Father, descending from heaven to earth so that we may be God's children as his brothers and sisters? He is our home. He is the open house and he is the bread and wine on the table which is spread for us. He is the gospel of God, the good news of what God is and does for us. He is God's word, spoken to us now, here and today, and we are called to take it to heart now, here, today and without delay. Thus to believe in the gospel of God is to believe in him and to repent is to trust him, to return home and to follow him. This is the true Christmas celebration: that we pay heed to the message and to the command, that we do not postpone action, but believe in him right now. May God grant us all this true Christmas celebration! May he grant this grace to many, to all men, to the whole world which stands in profound need of hearing the good news and the command, of believing in the gospel and through it in Jesus Christ! May all thereby truly repent, joyfully return to him and celebrate Christmas! Amen.

Yes Lord, our God and Father, grant that many, that all, that we ourselves may celebrate Christmas by returning humbly and gratefully, with joy and confidence to him whom thou hast sent us and in whom thou hast come among us. Take away from us all the vain things that have become useless and can, must and will fall from us now that the hour strikes and thy beloved Son, our Lord and Saviour, enters into our hearts and puts them in order.

Have mercy on all who do not, or not yet, acknowledge thee and thy kingdom, who may have known thee but have long since forgotten, misunderstood or even denied thee. Have mercy upon humanity in its present distress, anxiety and foolishness. Have mercy in particular on us for the Hungarian tragedy. Enlighten the thoughts of all those in authority, in the West as in the East, who seemingly do not know their course. Grant to the leaders and to the representatives of the people, to the magistrates, teachers and civil servants, and to the journalists the insights and incisiveness they need for responsibly doing their work. Give those who are to preach during this Christmas season the right, the necessary and the helpful words. Open the ears and hearts of those who listen. Comfort and encourage those who lie sick in body and soul in hospitals, in mental institutions and elsewhere. Comfort the prisoners, the distressed, abandoned and despaired with the only effective help, the clarity of thy word and the secret work of thy Holy Spirit.

We are grateful to know that we do not pray in vain, and never will. We are grateful for the light which thou madest to shine in the darkness and which the darkness comprehended not.

We are thankful that thou art our God and we are thy people. Amen.

THE CRIMINALS WITH HIM

Before the Lord's Supper on Good Friday 1957

O Lord, our God! We are met today to commemorate the fact that thy masterful and fatherly plan with the world and with ourselves has been carried out when thou didst permit our Lord Jesus Christ to be imprisoned that we may be free, to be declared guilty that our guilt may be taken away, to suffer that we may have joy, to be put to death that we may have life eternal.

Left to ourselves we are lost. None of us deserved to be rescued, not one. Yet in thy great majesty and mercy thou hast made common cause with our misery and our sin in order to lift us up. How else can we show our gratitude than by comprehending and acknowledging this mighty deed?

This can only happen when the same living Saviour who suffered for us, was crucified, died and was buried, now enters into our midst. Only when he speaks to our hearts and consciences, opening them to thy love and teaching us wholly to trust in thee and to live on thy love alone.

Humbly yet confidently we would ask that this may come to pass in the power of thy Holy Spirit.

'Our Father . . .'

My dear brothers and sisters, I should like to invite you, before I begin my sermon, to read for yourselves the story of Good Friday, the story of the suffering and death of Jesus Christ, as it is recorded in the four Gospels. Why don't you read it today and again and again? If we meditate and understand it rightly, this story contains the whole history of the world and, what is more, of God's dealing with man and hence of our dealings with God, including the life history of each of us here. I would need more than a half-hour were I to give an adequate summary of this history, let alone an insight into its complexity. Let me therefore select just one sentence for our meditation together. It is written in Luke 23.33.

They crucified him with the criminals, one on either side of him.

'They crucified him *with the criminals*'. Which is more amazing, to find Jesus in such bad company, or to find the criminals in such good company? As a matter of fact, both are true! One thing is certain: here they hang all three, Jesus and the criminals, one at the right and one at the left, all three exposed to the same public abuse, to the same interminable pain, to the same slow and irrevocable death throes. Like Jesus, these two criminals had been arrested somewhere, locked up and sentenced by some judge in the course of the previous few days. And now they hang on their crosses with him and find themselves in solidarity and fellowship with him. They are linked in a common bondage never again to be broken, just as the nails that fastened them to the piece of wood would never break. It was as inescapable for them as it was for him. It was a point of no return for them as for him. There remained only the shameful, painstricken present and the future of their approaching death. (Strangely enough, there are many paintings of Jesus' crucifixion where the two criminals are lost to sight. It would perhaps be more appropriate not to represent Jesus' death at all. But if it is done, then the two thieves on the right and on the left must not be left out. In any painting or representation where they are absent, an important, even an essential, element is missing.)

They crucified him with the criminals. Do you know what this implies? Don't be too surprised if I tell you that this was the first Christian fellowship, the first certain, indissoluble and indestructible Christian community. Christian community is manifest wherever there is a group of people close to Jesus who are with him in such a way that they are directly and unambiguously affected by his promise and assurance. These may hear that everything he is, he is for them, and everything he does, he does for them. To live by this promise is to be a Christian community. The two criminals were the first certain Christian community.

True, there existed before a vacillating, doubting community around Jesus. It was made up of disciples whom Jesus had called, who had wandered up and down Galilee with him and had followed him into Jerusalem, who had heard all his words and witnessed all his deeds. But what happened in the Garden of Gethsemane? 'So, could you not watch with me one hour?' No, they could not and they would not watch with him. They simply fell asleep while he watched and prayed alone. And what happened when the police came to fetch him? 'Then all the disciples forsook him and fled.' And what about Peter whom the Roman Catholic Church venerates up to the present as the first Pope? When a maid pointed to him in the courtyard of the High Priest, saying: 'This man also was with him', the great Peter denied: 'Woman, I do not know him.' And three times he thus spoke until the cock crowed for the third time. There was even Judas who betrayed the Master for thirty pieces of silver! Indeed there existed a Christian community before the two criminals. But what a wavering community it was!

The two criminals who at this hour were crucified with him had probably never heard of him before and were certainly no believing converts, no saints. Far from it! The opposite is true! But in this hour they could not abandon him, they could not sleep. Willingly or not, they were forced to watch with him many long hours on the cross. Nor could they escape his dangerous company. They could not very well deny him, being publicly exposed as his companions. This is how they were in fact the first certain Christian community! He and they, they and he were bound together, were not and are not to be separated in all eternity. Great things had to pass before Peter and the rest of the disciples joined this first Christian community. And when they did so, they could only 'get in line behind' the two criminals who were already first, and up there in front, with Jesus on Golgotha.

Before we take another look at these two criminals, we must say a word about Jesus together with whom they were exposed to the same abuse, the same pain and the same death throes. He was the principal actor, the hero of Good Friday, the head of this first Christian community. And now we are told that he was crucified. By whom? The hangmen, the Roman soldiers, obeying the order of Pilate, the governor. Pilate had been pressured by the church dignitaries of Jerusalem, they in turn had been mightily supported by the crowd shouting: 'crucify, crucify!'

What was happening here? Apparently the same thing that was happening to the two criminals. On account of his deeds and words a man had become unbearable for his fellowmen and they sent him from life to death, making him innocuous, extinguishing his life. Jesus would not have been himself, and his adversaries would not have been themselves, had they acted differently and not done this to him. Thus Jesus suffered the same lot which, for particular reasons, the two criminals had to endure (incidentally, a not uncommon or extraordinary human fate). Jesus was with them and they were with him. It has been rightly said that other people have been even more tormented by their fellowmen and have suffered harder pain than Jesus did on the cross—

be it at war, in concentration camps, or on the sickbed. But this is beside the point, for Jesus' sufferings were but the outward and visible sign of an inward event.

Through the visible suffering and death of this man Jesus an invisible event took place which did not and could not happen through the suffering and death of the two criminals nor, for that matter, of any other human being. Why not? Because Jesus, and he alone, was this man: a man like us, yet at the same time different from us because in him God himself was present and at work. The Roman centurion described this when he cried out after Jesus had died: 'Truly, this was a son of God!'

Who was God, and what did he do through the suffering and death of this man Jesus? The apostle Paul has summed it up in one sentence: 'He was in Christ reconciling the world unto himself' (2 Corinthians 5.19). I shall try to explain this to you in a few words.

It so happened that in this man Jesus God himself came into the world, which he had created and against all odds still loved. He took human nature upon himself and became man, like the rest of us, in order to put an end to the world's fight against him and also against itself, and to replace man's disorder by God's design. In Jesus God hallowed his name, made his kingdom come, his will done on earth as it is in heaven, as we say in the Lord's Prayer. In him he made manifest his glory and, amazingly enough, he made it manifest for our salvation. To accomplish this, he not only bandaged, but healed the wounds of the world; he helped mankind not only in part and temporarily, but radically and for good in the person of his beloved Son; he delivered us from evil and took us to his heart as his children. Thereby we are all permitted to live, and to live eternally.

It happened through this man on the cross that God cancelled out and swept away all our human wickedness, our pride, our anxiety, our greeds and our false pretences, whereby we had continually offended him and made life difficult, if not impossible, for ourselves and for others. He crossed out what had made our life fundamentally terrifying, dark and distressing—the life of health and of sickness, of happiness and of unhappiness, of the highborn and of the lowborn, of the rich and of the poor, of the free and of the captive. He did away with it. It is no longer part of us, it is behind us. In Jesus God made the day break after the long night and spring come after the long winter.

All these things happened in that one man. In Jesus, God took upon himself the full load of evil; he made our wickedness his own; he gave himself in his dear Son to be defamed as a criminal, to be accused, condemned, delivered from life unto death, as though he himself, the Holy God, had done all the evil we human beings did and do. In giving himself in Jesus Christ, he reconciled the world unto himself; he saved us and made us free to live in his everlasting kingdom; he removed the burden and took it upon himself. He the innocent took the place of us the guilty. He the mighty took the place of us the weak. He the living One took the place of us the dying.

This, my dear friends, is the invisible event that took place in the suffering and death of the man hanging on the middle cross on Golgotha. This is reconciliation: his damnation our liberation, his defeat our victory, his mortal pain the beginning of our joy, his death the birth of our life. We do well to remember that this is what those who put him to death really accomplished. They did not know what they did. These deluded men and women accomplished by their evil will and deed that good which God had willed and done with the world and for the world, including the crowd of Jerusalem.

Let us now go back to the two criminals who were crucified with Jesus according to God's will and deed. We do not know their names. We know nothing about their lives, of their misdoings and crimes. We do not know whether they could plead attenuating circumstances, or whether their guilt was even greater than we may think. We only know that the thieves were condemned, 'receiving', as one of them admitted, 'the due reward of our deeds'. We know above all that, without their consent and against their wishes, they were in fact crucified with him, with Jesus. No one before and no one afterwards has witnessed so directly and so closely God's act of reconciliation, God's glory and the redemption of the world, as these two thieves. True, only one of them acknowledged who Jesus was and what he did in his suffering and death for all men—the thief not excluded. His companion, as it is later recorded in the Gospels, shared in the general, blind and hollow mockery. Why did he not, if he really was the Christ, the Son of God, help himself and them? This is certainly an important and notable difference between the two criminals. But we shall not dwell on it today. For the difference is not important enough to invalidate the promise given so clearly, so urgently to both of them, indeed without distinction.

Consider the fact: Jesus died precisely for these two criminals who were crucified on his right and on his left and went to their death with him. He did not die for the sake of a good world, he died for the sake of an evil world, not for the pious, but for the godless, not for the just, but for the unjust, for the deliverance, the victory and the joy of all, that they might have life. These two companions were evidently and undeniably criminals, evil people, god-less people, unjust people. And he, like them, was condemned and crucified as a lawbreaker, a criminal. All three were under the same verdict.

Consider furthermore: 'My body which is broken for you! My blood which is shed for you!' These are Jesus' words at the Last Supper. How could these words be understood before his death? But now it is achieved, now his body is broken, his blood shed. The two thieves witnessed this breaking and shedding. And how did they witness it? They participated in this act not as mere spectators. In community with him, in the indissoluble bond uniting them, their own evil, sad and gloomy life was spent, and their own blood, clotted by many passions, was shed. What witnesses they were! How directly and closely these two not only saw with their eyes and heard with their ears but experienced in their flesh and in their own dying hearts: 'broken for you, shed for you!'

And let us consider above all that God's mighty deed to his glory and our salvation, his victory for the salvation of the world was accomplished through the event which took place at their side, even in their own existence. He who has overcome death, the King of Life, was the poor suffering servant whose dying gasp mingled with theirs. He who was on the road to the Kingdom, to the proclamation of his sovereignty, to the resurrection from the dead on the third day, was the same who went to death with them! Were they not therefore in turn, even in their darkest hour, on the road to the same destination? 'But if we have died with Christ, we believe that we shall also live with him' wrote the apostle Paul (Romans 6.8). Now, these two thieves literally died with Christ, and theirs was the assurance that they were also literally to live with him.

Did they accept this miracle, understand it, believe it? Let us leave this question open. This much is certain, that the promise was meant for them, that they were covered by this promise, that they received and possessed it, that they were allowed to suffer and to die with him. This promise is given and is valid wherever men may suffer and die as criminals with Jesus. This promise and nothing else constitutes the Christian community and makes man a Christian. These two criminals were the first two who, suffering and dying with Jesus, were gathered by this promise into the Christian fold.

I said that Peter and the remaining disciples could only 'get in line behind' the two criminals who were first and up front. This is true for men of all times. Christian community exists only where the promise is heard and believed. The promise is given only to crucified criminals, who are utterly compromised before God and before men, who move relentlessly toward the end and cannot escape this destiny by their own doing. For men like these Jesus died. And mark this: precisely these, and these only, are worthy to go to the Lord's Supper.

And now, dear friends, we are not asked in the least if we want to be such people, thank God. We are such people, all of us— you in this house which is called a prison, with all the burden that brought you here and with your particular experiences in this place—those others of us outside who have different experiences and yet are, believe me, in the same predicament. In reality we all are these people, these crucified criminals. And only one thing matters now. Are we ready to be told what we are? Are we ready to hear the promise given to the condemned, to 'get in line behind'? 'God opposes the proud, but gives grace to the humble.' Those receive the promise who regard themselves as neither so exalted nor so debased that they cannot 'get in line behind' the two criminals who were first on Golgotha. May God give us all the grace to do so! May he help us to use this grace rightly! May he bless us all as we in this freedom go to his table now! Amen.

O Lord our God, merciful and almighty Father! How thou dost love this evil world that thou hast willed to send thine only begotten Son on such a strange journey to save the world and us with it! This and nothing else has been thy pleasure, and this and nothing else shall be our pleasure as well. If only through him and in communion with him we find freedom, only through the depth we reach the height, only through suffering joy, only through death life, then we shall accept this as thy good and holy design.

Grant again and again that some come to recognize thy way with Jesus and with ourselves and thus may find peace according to thy will; here in this prison house and wherever the death of our Lord Jesus Christ is remembered and even where it is not remembered, in the whole world. Thou hast access to man which is unknown to us, but is clearly visible in thy sight.

In this assurance we bring before thee the sick and the weary, the poor and the distressed, those who have lost their way. In this assurance we ask for the Spirit of truth to be with those in church and state who bear the heavy responsibility to debate, to counsel, to decide, to judge and to command. We ask that thy Spirit be with labour and with management, with teachers and students, with the writers of books and newspapers, and with their readers.

We all stand in need of prayer and of intercession for each other when we face the cross of Jesus our Lord. Holy and forbearing thou art to assure us that no sincere prayer will remain unheard.

We thank thee that Jesus lives and that we may live with him. Finally we thank thee that we, as a token of this promise, may share together in the Lord's Supper. Amen.

ALL!

22 September 1957

O Lord, our God! Thou wilt that men, including us in this house today, hear thy word of comfort and exhortation, call on thee and praise thy name. Thou hast so decided in thy undeserved kindness. For what are we before thee and for thee? But thou hast called us, and we have heard thy call. And now we are assembled here: thy creatures in all the weakness, darkness and rebellion that is ours; thy children whom thou lovest even though we scarcely love thee and certainly do not love thee rightly; thy congregation, a strange crowd here as everywhere in the world. Yet thou wilt be present and at work in our midst.

Because we utterly depend on thy care we wait for thee, for thy good and Holy Spirit and his gifts. Brighten this hour, let it be pleasing in thy sight, and helpful and fruitful for us! Grant that our human doings, our prayers, our sermon, and our hymns, bespeak power and truth, come from heart and go to heart. Be thou our master, our teacher, our mighty and good Lord over all thoughts that move each one of us in this hour of worship.

In the name of thy dear Son in whom thou hast shown us and wilt evermore show us thy free grace, we pray as he has prayed before us, 'Our Father . . .'

For God has made all men prisoners, that he may have mercy upon all.

MY DEAR BROTHERS AND SISTERS, you have surely noticed right away that our text is not very easy to understand. I frankly confess that I myself, having read time and again Paul's letter to the Romans in the course of my rather long life, am still wrestling with these words, as with so many passages of this letter and of the entire Bible. The text stimulates my thinking ever anew. I am certain that in it, like in a very hard shell, there lies hidden a most precious pearl. May God let me give you a glimpse of what it means!

'*That he may have mercy on all!*' This second phrase shall be our starting point. It looks like a mountain which we cannot climb, in our thoughts or in a sermon—a mountain from which we can only climb down. The apostle Paul himself could not have started out with the affirmation that 'God has made all men prisoners' had he not first and foremost known and pondered the affirmation 'that he may have mercy upon all'. We, too, must begin with this second phrase.

We would indeed forget Christmas, Good Friday and Easter, we would dismiss Jesus Christ himself, were we not to follow this order. He who knows Jesus knows that it is both impossible to dismiss him, and imperative to begin at all times in our thoughts and in our life with him, and with him alone, just as the alphabet has no other beginning than the letter A. We must start with the fact that God had mercy and will have mercy on *all*—that his will and work are determined and governed by his compassion. This he proved in Jesus Christ not only by words, but by the mightiest of his deeds. He gave himself for us in his dear Son and became man, our brother. This is the mighty deed and through it the word of God's mercy on all has been spoken. We may and we must stick to this truth and ever anew begin with it.

God has mercy on us. He says 'yes' to us, he wills to be on our side, to be our God against all odds. Indeed against all odds, because we do not deserve this mercy, because, as we rightly suppose, he should say 'no' to us all. But he does not say 'no'; he says 'yes'. He is not against us; he is for us. This is God's mercy.

Contrary to human mercy even in its kindest expression, God's mercy is almighty. It is almightily saving and helpful. It brings light, peace and joy. We need not be afraid that it might be limited or have strings attached. His 'yes' is unequivocal, never to be reversed into 'no'.

Since God's mercy is divine and not human, it is poured out on all men, as emphasized in our text. In his letter to the Romans Paul interprets this mercy by insisting that it is extended to the Jews *and* the Gentiles—to those near, or at least nearer, to God and to those far away from him—to the so-called pious and the so-called unbelievers—to the so-called good and the so-called evil people—truly to *all*. God has mercy on all, though on each one in his own way. God's mercy is such as it is described in the parable of the lost sheep, of the lost coin, and of the prodigal son.

Let us pause here for a moment. As according to God's holy word, spoken in Jesus Christ, he has mercy on all, each one of you may and shall repeat—not after me, but after him—'I am one of them'. God has mercy on me and will have mercy on me. The one great sin for anyone right now would be to think: 'This is not meant for me. God does not have mercy on me and will not have mercy on me.' Or even worse: 'I do not need mercy. I do not want it!' This would be the one great sin which we had rather not commit this morning. God has mercy on all, including you and me. As a result you and I may and shall live from this 'yes' spoken to all men, spoken to us, and live here and now!

But wait a minute! Because according to the word that God has spoken in Jesus Christ he has mercy on all, we may and we must repeat in our hearts: 'Among all people on whom God has mercy are this man and that woman, this fellow-creature beside me, in front of me or behind, whom I don't like to remember. Perhaps he did me wrong, or I am not pleased with him for other reasons. Perhaps I must even consider him as my enemy, and myself as his enemy.' God has mercy on all—even on this other fellow! His 'yes' is valid also for him. The one great sin from which we shall try to escape this morning is to exclude anyone from the 'yes' of God's mercy. In our thoughts, words and deeds we may live, and we must live, with each neighbour as with one to whom God is compassionate. We not only pray 'Lord, have mercy on me!' We also pray 'Lord have mercy on us, have mercy on us all!' This has been the prayer of the Christian Church from the very beginning, and this is the true prayer for us today.

This is what needs very briefly to be said about God's mercy. This is the height from which we may proceed, come what may.

But from these heights we are asked to descend into the depths of what we have heard. That he may have mercy on all, *God has made all men prisoners of disobedience*. Prisoners! I may dispense with explaining the most obvious meaning of this term in a house where there are so many closed doors. But man may be a prisoner of quite different and much worse kind than you are here. Prisoner of a sorrow that once befell him and now poisons his heart and life! Prisoner of resentment, anger or hatred, perhaps rightfully directed against some people who gave him offence! Prisoner of a dismal tendency or habit which since his younger days he has been unable to shake off! Prisoner of a depressing illness of the body, like the people in the hospital over there! Quite a large number of our contemporaries are prisoners of mutual distrust, of the bitter feud between East and West, between the so-called 'free world' and the world of so-called 'socialism'. And all of us may feel like prisoners of anxiety, of the great and truly frightening fear of a third world war and of the bombs that people intend to drop on each other on that occasion. Lastly—I could have mentioned it first—we are all prisoners of the limitations of our one and only life, which is so short, prisoners of the limitations of our birth and our approaching death.

Nevertheless, these prisoners of various kinds are locked up behind doors that may open one day, that already have slits through which they can peek. Man even manages, at least in his thoughts, to dispel the harsh fact that he must die.

There remains, however, one prison whose door has no slits or peeping holes. 'God has made all men prisoners of disobedience.' What does this mean? What kind of imprisonment is this?

We are all prisoners because God in his infallible knowledge knows who and what we are, and by his unmistakable word reveals our true being as fundamentally disobedient. Not only disobedient to parents and teachers and superiors, as we were often enough in our youth; nor disobedient to human custom and human law, or to our own conscience. True, we all were and still are disobedient in this respect, even though not evenly, not altogether, and not ultimately. But God knows and tell us—this is the imprisonment—that we are disobedient *before him* and *to him*. What does this mean?

It does not necessarily imply that one has to be an atheist who straightforwardly thinks and affirms that there is no God. I dare say there are very few such outspoken atheists, and these may not even be of the worst kind. Disobeying God means, whether we believe in him or not, that we let him be the 'man upstairs' and reserve for ourselves, in our hearts and minds and lives, the right to go our own ways. Disobeying God means that we affirm in our innermost hearts and with our outward life that there is no God. This is precisely what we are doing all the time.

It is the disobedience, the rebellion and revolt, the attempt at an impossible ascent in the mountains. He who tries the impossible makes himself impossible, and is doomed to perish. God knows that we attempt the impossible, that we are these foolish mountain-climbers, and he tells us so. This is the door without slits on which we pound in vain. There is no denial of our ultimate disobedience. It is as true as God is God and man is man.

The text insists that God has made *all* men prisoners of disobedience. *All*, including me, the preacher of this Sunday sermon? Yes, including me! Including the good or at least the better fellows among you? Yes, including them! Including the best people that ever lived or may live on earth? Yes, including these! The all-knowing God declares that all, each one in his own way, yet each and all, are prisoners of disobedience.

We must again pause for a moment. Because this is our common predicament, none shall secretly exempt himself; none shall point to the other fellow as a more obvious target; none shall think of himself as an exception, if only a half-exception or a quarter-exception. My brothers and sisters, everything depends on our readiness not to escape at this point. Not only because there is no escape—but because an escape would work to our disadvantage. Our peace and our joy, our salvation in time and eternity are here determined. We are not to deny, but to acknowledge, not to mutiny against, but to confess: God has made me and you *prisoners of disobedience.*

God's purpose is not to debase us nor to put us to shame. I repeat: God is not against us, he is for us. As a great saint has rightly put it, the Saviour is no kill-joy. The arms of his eternal love, if I may say so, are already outstretched when he makes us prisoners of disobedience. He does so in order to have mercy on all. He keeps us, the prisoners of disobedience, together like a shepherd his flock. He keeps us in line and holds us in check. He places us on the very spot where his mercy is operative and manifest, he gathers us as his people, transfers us into a community of our Lord Jesus Christ.

For he has made Jesus Christ our Saviour by delivering his own beloved and obedient Son to disobedience and death in our place. 'For our sake he made him to be sin who knew no sin', says the apostle Paul elsewhere, in an equally difficult passage. And Jesus Christ was obedient to God by not rebelling against his will, but by submitting to it. We are called to belong to him, to share in God's eternal mercy poured out in him, to rejoice in our salvation through him, and to live in the power of this mercy and this salvation. Therefore, we have no other choice but to submit to God's design to make us all prisoners of disobedience.

This leads us, in conclusion, to some questions and their answers.

You yearn for new courage, for courage to be? You may and even ought to do so. True courage to be is the courage to be humble, consciously to participate in the divine mercy as a prisoner of disobedience. Thus you become and remain a courageous man.

You yearn for your right? All of us yearn for our rights! And you shall obtain it from God and before God, even though you are wrong before men and in your own conscience. But you will become aware of your right before God at the very moment you confess, without reservation and in complete honesty, to be wrong before this very God.

You yearn to rise again? This also is legitimate and appropriate. But I have to ask you one other question: Did you ever reach the depth? Not only the depth of any inward or outward misery, but the depth where man must acknowledge that he can no longer help himself, that no man can help him, that there is absolutely no help save God's mercy? In this depth, God's mercy has already reached out for you, has already found you, and you will experience that it will lift you to the highest heights.

Finally, *you yearn for joy?* Yes, we all yearn for joy, and rightly so. Real, lasting joy has a very quiet, unobtrusive and hidden beginning. Joy is born when you renounce any attempt to be something more than one among all those whom God has made prisoners of disobedience, that he may have mercy on all. Joy is born when you submit to both God's mercy and God's imprisoning, without resistance. Amen.

God, Father, Son and Holy Ghost! Forbid that we depart without thy loving and severe word accompanying us, each one to his place; into his particular experiences, concerns, sorrows and expectations, into this Sunday and into this coming week! Be and remain present and at work in this house, and with all its inmates. Restrain all evil spirits which threaten to overpower us! Keep the light burning which so often is about to go out.

We ask this for all people gathered today in thy name here and elsewhere, and for the world in need of a courageous, clear and joyful Christian witness. We commend to thy faithfulness in particular our loved ones. We ask thee to grant wisdom to the powerful of this world who are in charge of keeping justice and peace on thy behalf; sober vision to those who day by day write our newspapers; love and perseverance to all parents and teachers; joyful forbearance in all families and homes; open, brotherly hearts and hands towards the poor and the lonely; relief and patience for the sick; hope of eternal life for the dying.

We are thankful that we may bring all these our concerns before thee, who knowest much better than we do what we need, and what is best for thy struggling Church and for the bewildered world; thou canst help and wilt help far more abundantly than all that we ask or think.

We are in thy hand. We bend under thy judgment and we praise thy mercy. Amen.

GOD'S GOOD CREATION

6 October 1957[1]

Dear Heavenly Father! We are thankful for thy permission and commandment to come together in this hour to adore thee, to proclaim thy word, to listen to it, and to receive it in our hearts.

Yet we are not wont to come before thee in a way pleasing to thee and salutary for ourselves. Therefore we sincerely and humbly beseech thee to be with us and to take thy cause in thine own hands! Cleanse our speaking and our listening! Open and enlighten our hearts and our minds! Awaken and strengthen our willingness to acknowledge thee and our readiness to let thee establish thy right among us! Let us breathe the fresh air of thy Spirit, enabling us to return to our work tomorrow with forbearance, love and joy renewed!

To thy presence and guidance we commend, together with ourselves, all the people of our neighbourhood, of our town and country and everywhere. Thou hast ways and means to speak to each one of them and to comfort and admonish them. Do not abandon them nor us, we beseech thee, but let there be light where darkness now reigns, let there be peace where there is now strife, let there be courage and confidence where now sorrow and anxiety hold men in their grip. Hearken to our supplications, not because we deserve thy mercy, but for Jesus Christ's sake in whom in thy incomprehensible mercy thou hast deemed us from all eternity to be thy children. Amen.

[1] Sermon preached in the Bruderholzkapelle, Basel.

For everything created by God is good, and nothing is to be rejected if it is received with thanksgiving; for then it is consecrated by the word of God and prayer. I TIMOTHY 4.4-5

DEAR FRIENDS, everything created by God—'every creature of God', as other translations have it—is *good*. This is what our text affirms. It does not say that everything is good. Frankly, not everything is good. The things created and being created by man are all more or less corrupted by our lies and our laziness, by our conceit and our malice. What is good in human works refers to remaining vestiges in them of God's good creation, of what God created good. Or, to put it differently, it refers to the privilege we enjoy to live in God's forgiveness and to make operative, or at least to reflect, a measure of his redeeming grace in whatever we do.

Every creature of God is wholly and unreservedly good. If you will take the time to read our text once more at home, you will see that the chapter begins with the relationship between man and woman and continues with eating and drinking—two realms where human depravity has usually reared its ugly head. Yet it is maintained that everything created by God is good. What is more, the affirmation is valid for the whole of God's creation. It includes all nature with its powers, even the seemingly dark and threatening ones like atomic power. It also includes the whole man such as he is, not only his soul but his body and all its organs as well, all human gifts and potentialities, even those wherein man is a mystery to himself. It extends to the whole of humanity at all times and in all places, however dim and dark these may appear to us. It even applies to the whole spectrum of human life, including its impermanence, its fleeting qualities and its finiteness. Everything created by God is good. Such an affirmation is bound to stir up questions and doubts. But let us put these aside for a while and quite simply be told that everything created by God is good. We read it already in the beginning of the story of creation. 'And God saw everything that he had made, and behold, it was very good.'

Good! The true meaning of the Greek word used in this context is 'beautiful'. How strange that the Bible should say that what God created is beautiful! The meaning, in fact, is that everything created by God is good, is right, is well-ordered and therefore is beneficial. Why beautiful? We may give a very simple answer. Everything created by God is beautiful because he created it. He intended all creation to give glory to their maker, especially man whom he made in his own image. The New Testament adds precision to this answer. The opening words of the Gospel according to St John, in accordance with similar texts, tell us that all things were made through him— through the Word of God which is called Jesus Christ—and without him, without Jesus Christ, was not anything made that was made. Interpreting these passages we are bold to say that everything created by God is good because he, Jesus Christ, is the origin and purpose of God's creation and of everything created by him, because in all of God's creatures we encounter Jesus Christ as their innermost mystery. This is why everything created by God is called beautiful and good!

This gives a very special connotation and significance to the little word 'good'. Everything created by God is good, we must now say, because it contains and reflects God's mercy, free will, and royal power to help and to save us, and to draw us unto him. This is Jesus Christ! God's creation is good because his love and hence his glory is the mystery of existence. God willed all that is to serve him, and us to serve his love and our salvation. Everything made by him is to be likened to a house built and furnished by him to welcome us, his beloved children, and to give us shelter.

There is nothing to be rejected in God's creation, nothing ugly, nothing evil, nothing dangerous, nothing to be feared, to be shunned, to be avoided by us. Should God reject what he himself created? Should he reject what he willed and created in the purpose which culminates in Jesus Christ? Should he command us to shun and to avoid his own creation?

True, there are a great many things to be rejected, things ugly, evil and dangerous. Our life and the world are full of them. However, what is to be rejected is surely not created by God. The very nature of things to be rejected may be defined as not being willed, and not being created by God. Their distinctive mark, therefore, lies in their alienation from Jesus Christ and his grace; they serve neither God nor ourselves and do not contribute to the building up of the household of God. Originating in our misguided hearts and minds, they are the work of the Evil One who fails as another creator. Rejected and denied by God and relegated to his left, these are the very things we are ordered to reject and to shun. However, the existence of these things to be rejected—and their number is legion—does not alter the fact that everything created by God is good. We cannot change it; nor can the devil.

The imprint of God's good creation in our lives, and in the world around us, is always and everywhere recognizable, in as much as we may and even must receive with thanksgiving what is offered to our experience.

What is the meaning of 'thanksgiving'? The Greek word used in the Bible in this context signifies 'Eucharist'. This term carries a double meaning which is of the utmost importance in examining our question.

Thanksgiving, Eucharist, is used on the one hand to describe the attitude and action of a person who has been encountered by God's grace. He acknowledges grace for what it truly is and thereby receives it in the way it may and must be received: not as a treasure sought and finally found, coveted and finally won, let alone conquered and then appropriated as a trophy, but as an unexpected and undeserved gift freely offered. When we give thanks we acknowledge that our thoughts and our words, the things we have done and left undone, are determined by this gift, that they respond and correspond to grace and even reflect it. We cannot give thanks for the things to be rejected, precisely because they have nothing in common with grace. Rather we grab them like a robber grabs his prey or like a beast gulps at his food. The opposite holds equally true. Once we recognize and accept God's good creation as his grace and receive it with thanksgiving, it is not to be rejected.

But Thanksgiving, Eucharist, has still another meaning. The term has been used since the beginning of the Christian Church to designate the Lord's Supper, the communion of the people gathered around the table to eat real bread and drink real wine, really to make use of the things created by God, of bread and wine. Of this community the crucified and risen Christ himself is both the host and the food, giving himself, his own life, for us to eat and drink so that we may live. What is there to be feared or shunned? The things to be rejected, which we can only fear and shun, cannot be received as we receive the Lord's Supper. It is certainly not Jesus Christ who offers himself as bread and wine in them. The reverse holds again true. What we may receive in the manner of the Lord's Supper is God's good creation; it is not to be rejected nor shunned because it is not to be feared.

To sum up, wherever we may accept our lives and the world, our thoughts, desires and hopes, our human relationships, our joys and also our sorrows *with thanksgiving*—as we receive God's grace, as we receive the Lord's Supper—there everything is according to God's design, there we are presented with God's good creation. We have a green light, we need not be afraid, we are allowed to live in the freedom of the children of God, which is true obedience. The obedience of the children of God is borne out in this freedom.

Let me add a last word, which may well be the most important. It is a peculiar mark of our life and of the world around us that we are constantly entangled in a strange contradiction. On the one hand we are presented at all times and in all things with God's good creation, with his beautiful creation, where there is nothing to be rejected, where we may truly rejoice because everything is right, where we may be free and hence obedient people, God's own children. On the other hand, however, we meet and are impressed by the things to be rejected, neither willed nor created by God, belonging entirely to the realm of darkness. These things are ever present and manifest themselves mightily, rising again and again out of the depth of our misguided hearts and minds, as an endless devilish threat.

It is therefore not at all self-evident that we, entangled in this contradiction, receive with thanksgiving God's good creation, nor that our life in this world is right and in order. Rather, it seems to be an amazing, an almost impossible, *exception* that we should recognize God's good creation for what it is—that we should receive it as grace with thanksgiving, as we do at the Lord's Supper—that we should be transformed by its impact into free and obedient human beings. Really, this is not self-evident!

The mystery is pierced through when our human existence, when we ourselves, 'are consecrated by the word of God and prayer'. What does this mean? It means that we participate in the great history highlighted by the very simple and yet totally incomprehensible event of God speaking with man and man being allowed and willing to speak with God. When this event —the word of God and prayer—happens, and happens in our lives, when this history involving God and man becomes the main thread running through the fabric of our life's history, then we are consecrated. The contradiction of human existence begins to resolve itself; slowly but steadily we are freed from the preponderance of things to be rejected and open up to the goodness of God's creation around us. Thus we wake up to give thanks as the free and obedient recipients of God's grace and of the Lord's Supper.

This great history involving God and man, in which our lives are sanctified by the word of God and prayer, is no other than the history of our Lord and Saviour Jesus Christ. He was and he is the true God speaking to man and the true man speaking to God. In him God calls us also, you and me, and again in him may we, you and I, respond to God. Whenever God's calling and man's response, as embodied in Jesus Christ, are manifest among us, in your life and mine, then we are consecrated. All other virtues like faith, love and hope, and human life lived in the power and under the guidance of the Holy Spirit, are but different words for the enactment of the great history of Jesus Christ in our life and its history. Our consecration by this encounter 'by the word of God and prayer', is then unconditionally and unquestionably the neverfailing source of our freedom, our obedience and our thanksgiving whereby we most certainly will recognize God's good creation.

May God open afresh this source of thankfulness for each one in his own life! May he make us willing gladly to quench our thirst at this source! May he renew our strength! May he grant us to hear him saying every day, every morning and evening anew, 'You are Christ's'! May he grant us to hear also his other message, 'Because you are Christians, because you belong to Christ, therefore everything is yours, God's whole, good creation, everything created good and beautiful by God!' Amen.

Lord, in thy infinite mercy thou hast given us our life and all we are and have and are capable of, and hast preserved it until this day. Forgive us any arbitrary or negligent use, any misuse which we have been guilty of since time immemorial, even in the course of the week that is now past, and indeed on this very Sunday. Keep us in thy care today and tomorrow!

Set us free from all dogged or lazy habits of work, from the tyranny of monotony, fashion and public opinion! Grant that we may go on hearing thy word, and give us courage and freedom to pray to thee. Convert us ever afresh to the thanksgiving of heart and hands so that we may not perish, but have everlasting life.

Accomplish this work of thy good and Holy Spirit in every corner of every land—among the big people and the small people—among employers and employees—among the sick and the healthy—among the affluent and the indigent—among those who must decide and command and those who must obey—among our officials and judges and among the lawbreakers and convicts—among the clergy and missionaries, among Christians and non-Christians whom we are called and willing to serve!

Lord have mercy upon us, upon thy people, upon thy creation! We praise and magnify thee, knowing that thy mercy is without end and thy power without limit. Once again we call upon thee with the prayer of thy Son: 'Our Father . . .'

THE GREAT DISPENSATION

At a Basel University Christmas Service, 1957

O Lord, our God! *Thou hast humbled thyself that we may be exalted. Thou hast become poor that we may be rich. Thou hast come to us to draw us to thee. Thou hast become man like us to make us partake of thine eternal life. All this thou hast done in thy free and undeserved compassion. This thou hast done in thy dear Son, our Lord and Saviour Jesus Christ.*

Lost in wonder before this mystery, we are met here to adore thee, to proclaim and to hear thy word. Yet we know that we lack the power to do it unless thou makest us free to lift up our hearts and minds to thee. Therefore we pray: Descend now into our midst! Reveal and open for us the way to thee by the power of thy Holy Spirit! Enable us to see with our own eyes the light that has come into the world, and to be thy witnesses in every act of our lives!

'Our Father . . .'

The Lord is at hand. Have no anxiety about anything, but in everything by prayer and supplication with thanksgiving let your requests be known to God.   PHILIPPIANS 4.5-6

DEAR FELLOWSTUDENTS, COLLEAGUES, FRIENDS, a good friend of mine wrote me from Holland a week ago to wish me for the Christmas season as much celebration and as little ceremonial as possible. I liked that. Yet I don't want to waste one minute in criticizing or decrying the many religious and secular Christmas ceremonies of a public or a private nature. Their questionable features are well enough known. Of one thing I am certain. Christmas is an occasion for celebrating, and not for ceremonial.

Celebrating! This suggests holy days and holidays. We think of vacations, of rest and relaxation, of pausing in the rough-and-tumble and fret of everyday life. In peace of mind we shall celebrate Christmas. Let us take special notice right here that Christmas is not a short-lived affair as holidays usually are. A true Christmas celebration is an event that penetrates our hearts and our lives. It takes possession of us and does not relinquish us any more. We breathe freely and no longer gasp. We are permanently freed from unrest.

This 'celebrating' is indicated by Paul when he says, *Have no anxiety about anything.* Dear friends, this is the announcement of the great Christmas holy day and holiday, of everlasting and complete vacations. We *shall* not be anxious? No, we *need* not be anxious! We can afford not to have anxiety about anything. We may accept this dispensation and make use of it. This is the true Christmas celebration, *Have no anxiety about anything.*

When we do have anxiety, we take ourselves so seriously as to imagine that we are able to solve the great problems of life by ourselves. We feel in duty bound to shoulder, like Atlas, the great burden of life and all the lesser loads, to manipulate them, master them and get them out of the way. We realize—don't

we?—that anxiety has a great deal to do with ceremonial.
When we are anxious, we get ceremonial. Where there is ceremonial, anxiety lurks backstage.

Burdens and questions of life—yes, they are real. We all want
so much to be happy, conceivably because we are somewhat
unhappy. This *is* a problem in our life. Another one is how to
discern our purpose in life, and how to live up to it. Still another
question is how I rate with the people around me. Am I suf-
ficiently esteemed? Do I get my due? How can I get along with
this fellowman or that one, how can I stand him, how can I
perhaps even help him? What about human existence? Is it
bearable, is there any sense in being born? A very serious question indeed! He who has never considered it shall go to Sartre
and Camus and learn from them how to take it seriously. What
is man's eternal destiny, his salvation or maybe his damnation?

Paul's comment on all these questions, including the last one,
is, *Have no anxiety about anything*. This is the great dispensation.
It does in no way deny the seriousness and genuineness of these
questions. It only asserts that we are freed from the compulsion
to tackle and solve these problems by ourselves. It is not your
business to procure your own happiness; it is not your business
to stake out the purpose and task of your life, even less to
determine whether or not you live up to it. Hands off! Quit
worrying about the limitations and the results of your work.
Furthermore, it is not up to you to make out your fellowman,
neither in terms of his shortcomings nor in terms of his achieve-
ments. And lastly, it is not up to you to decide whether human
existence is meaningful, let alone to gain eternal salvation or
damnation.

Have no anxiety! This is to have a good holiday, to pause and
breathe, to take it easy, definitely to enjoy vacations!

You ask perhaps how these comments relate to Christmas, to
the celebration of Christmas. They have a great deal, even

everything to do with it! For if it is truly deliverance from anxiety, if it is truly genuine, then this celebration is allowed and commanded by the message of our text. If it were not the celebration of Christmas, it would indeed be a dubious undertaking. It would betray a foolish, even a pernicious blindness to the seriousness and the burdens of life, of arbitrary and inexcusable frivolity, of existential hoax. Or it would denote a worn-out and irresponsible scepticism. God keep us from these 'celebrations' which are but manifestations of disguised anxiety! We can dispense with them, too!

The invitation to a genuine, anxiety-free celebration is extended by the Lord who is at hand. It is the Lord whose birth the angels announced to the shepherds at Bethlehem, he 'who is Christ the Lord in the city of David'. The Lord whose star is not only a thousand times but infinitely more important than the successful Russian sputnik and its unsuccessful American counterpart! The Lord of heaven and earth, the eternal God who deemed it not too high and not too low to become like us so that we may become his. The Lord who in his life and death as a man loved the world and reconciled it unto himself. The Lord who took upon himself all questions and all burdens of life, putting them out of the way to make us live with him and in him. 'Glory to God in the highest and peace on earth towards men with whom he is so infinitely well pleased!'

The Lord is at hand. Not, some comforts of religion are at hand; these are but another sign of man's inability to comfort himself. Nor is the Church at hand with its old and new teachings and theologies or with its orders and institutions and with its traditions. The Church's existence is validated not by witness to itself, but only by witness to the Lord who is not dead, but alive, who has not passed away and is past, but comes. He comes now and he comes not only to the other fellow, but to you and to me. 'Behold, I stand at the door and knock.'

The coming of this Lord is the mystery of the great dispensation. As the storms of spring thaw the ice and snow, and the fire kindles the tinder, the Lord wipes out our anxieties and sweeps them away. We need not care because we are taken care of, because we are rightfully released from the grip of anxiety, because it would be wrong to worry all the same.

You ask me: 'What remains to be done by us, the carefree?' With this question a new anxiety creeps in, disguised in proud defiance. It is stubborn yet violent, as if the best and most sacred qualities of human life came under attack. What odd creatures we are! We talk about our anxieties, they make us miserable, yet when the great dispensation is announced and we are told not to be anxious, then it becomes evident how much we appreciate, even treasure and nurture our worries and our own self in them. I shall never forget the phone call I once received from a good old friend of mine who dished out her complaints. She was suffering from asthma and depressions and I tried to comfort her with an old nursery rhyme:

> Der lieb Gott het recht an mi denkt, und het mer hit vyl Fraide
>   geschenkt
> Er b'hietet me and segnet me: s'isch hitte luschtig gsi!

The good Lord thought of me today, he gave me lots of fun,
He watches me and blesses me: my place is in the sun.

She interrupted most violently. 'No, the Lord did not think of me; no, I did not have lots of fun!' Her troubles were too dear to her heart, and she refused to get rid of them. It is, of course, also quite possible that I failed to convey to her the right word of comfort.

But, you will object, is this resistance to depart with our anxieties not appropriate and important at times? Let us suppose we avail ourselves of the great dispensation. Then what? The questions and burdens of life which our Lord has taken upon himself are still with us, casting their shadows about, although the anxiety is gone, melted like ice or burnt like tinder. Are we condemned to folding our hands in our lap and being idle? Would this be a respectable existence, a life worth living? Might not this state of suspense give birth to new anxieties?

No, we are not kept in abeyance. When the Lord is at hand and shuts the door to anxiety, he opens another door for us. He leads us on firm ground and proposes things and activities that are far better than worrying. Paul describes these 'far better things' as follows: *But in everything . . . let your requests be known to God.* This is what Christmas invites and encourages us to do as those whom our Lord saved and freed, and delivered from the prison of anxiety. God does not need to be told all our troubles and fears, but we, like children, may bring before him and talk over with him all our concerns, great and small, important or less important, intelligent or foolish. We may tell him how difficult life is, how we are puzzled by things and persons around us, above all where we have to blame ourselves for these difficulties and fail to get along with each other. We may indeed tell him all these things *in prayer*, in great and genuine humility; *in supplication*, in childlike insistence and trust; with *thanksgiving* for the knowledge that our Lord has already put aright man's disorder, and for the grace to come into his presence. All these are summed up in our *requests* that his countenance may not cease to shine upon us amidst the surrounding shadows, and that we never cease hoping for their dissipation, for the lifting of the fog and the veils that dim our vision. These are the 'far better things' awaiting us when we are delivered from anxiety.

Only *prayer*, then? Yes, only prayer! Have you ever really tried to cast all your cares before the Lord in fervent and insistent prayer? Not as a routine matter, but because the Lord is at hand? Have you ever (as you should) dared letting all your requests be known before God, praying as his brother, as his sister, as God's child? Whoever has tried and done this knows that such prayer, nothing but prayer, includes vigilant, steady and effective action. He is not afraid that prayer might not be sufficient. Rather, through prayer, he will be incited to bring his life, his thoughts, his words, and his deeds step by step into accordance with his supplications. He will make small and unassuming, yet very definite steps, confident and even gay steps despite bewilderment. In an unintentional and unforeseeable way, he will shed some light for others on this dark earth.

In this sense, let us celebrate Christmas joyfully. We may and we can do it; we have every reason to do it—*The Lord is nigh!* How can we *not* keep a joyful feast?

Dear Father through our Lord Jesus Christ! Put aright what we did wrong, including this imperfect worship service and the many other Christmas celebrations to which we look forward with understanding or foolish hearts! Thou art able to make water flow from the rock, to change water into wine, and to beget children of Abraham from these stones. Thou dost so in the unspeakable faithfulness which thou hast pledged to thy people and evidenced again and again. Thy lovingkindness shines through the gospel, and we may abide in it in all adversities of life. For this we give thee thanks, imploring thee not to let us harden our hearts against it. Keep stirring us from the sleep of indifference and from the bad dreams of our pious and impious passions and greeds! Never cease to lead us back to thy ways!

Restrain the folly of the cold war and the mutual threats whereby the community of men is exposed to mortal danger. Bestow upon the governments and upon those who mould public opinion new wisdom, patience and decisiveness that are so sorely needed for establishing and preserving the rights of all men on thy good earth! Grant, we beseech thee, that the work done in our city, in our churches, in our University and in our schools be not deprived of thy light and thy blessing, to the well-being of us all and to thy glory. Above all we pray today for the many whose Christmas joy is overshadowed: for the poor, known and unknown, for those ageing in loneliness, for the sick and the mentally ill, for the prisoners. May thy light brighten their days! Lastly, we entrust to thy care our loved ones near and afar, as well as ourselves, asking thee mercifully to extend thy hand over our life, and when the time comes, over our departing.

Lord, have mercy upon us! Thy name be praised, now and forever more. Amen.

REMEMBER THE LORD

O Lord, our God! Our years come and go. We ourselves live and die. But thou art forever. Thy kingdom and thy faithfulness, thy righteousness and thy mercy are without beginning and end. Thou art likewise the origin and destination of our lives. Thou art the judge of our thoughts, words and deeds.

We acknowledge with contrite hearts today that we have so often forgotten thee, denied thee, offended thee. And yet we are comforted and enlightened anew by thy assurance that thou art our Father and we are thy children, because thy dear Son Jesus Christ was made man, died and rose for us, and is our brother.

We give thee thanks that we may once more announce and hear these glad tidings on this last Sunday of the year. Make us free, O Lord, to say what is right and rightly to receive it, that this hour may further thy glory and the peace and salvation of us all. Amen.

'Our Father . . .'

You shall remember the Lord your God, for it is he who gives you power.
DEUTERONOMY 8.18

MY DEAR BROTHERS AND SISTERS, how I wish I could
utter and you could hear this 'It is he!' in such a way that it
would shine brighter than a thousand suns, blinding our eyes
so we could perceive nothing else for a moment. Then our eyes
would be opened to an entirely fresh vision of God's eternity
surrounding our humanity, God's ways determining our human
ways, God's truth containing what we hold for truth, and God's
life sustaining our human lives.

But whether my preaching is good or bad, whether your
understanding is deep or shallow, what it is all about, what is
laid out before us and may be grasped by every man is this:
'It is he who gives you power!' You don't give power to yourself. No one else can give it to you. Not even the best of circumstances or the fulfilment of your highest dreams can give it to
you. It is he who gives you power.

This text stands in one of the most beautiful and moving
chapters of the Old Testament. I should like to invite you to
open your Bibles when you are alone again and reread it (it is
the 8th chapter of Deuteronomy). The text is addressed to the
people of Israel. The long and strenuous journey through the
desert is behind them, and the promised land of their forefathers
lies before their eyes. These people are now told: 'Do not
imagine you succeeded in this venture for yourselves! No, it is
the Lord, your God, who tested you in the wilderness and at
the same time sustained you. It is the Lord, your God, who has
given you this good land. Therefore you shall remember him.
It is he who gives you power.'

But now, let us hear this word quite directly addressed to
ourselves. For isn't it true that the journey which lies behind
us at the end of this year and the journeys of all previous years
somehow fit the description of this chapter? We too wandered

through 'the great and terrible wilderness, with its fiery serpents and scorpions and thirsty ground where there was no water'. And isn't it equally true that we are on the threshold of a future where things will be good, even very good, for us? It is a future where we all may sigh with relief, where we all shall be comforted and quickened. Likewise, we are all reminded in this moment of looking back and of looking ahead not to forget but to remember that it is he who gives us power. All the hardships we may have endured in the past would have been suffered in vain, and all the hope with which we look out into the promised future would be an illusion were we to forget, were we not to remember that it is he who gives us power. But why should we forget this truth? We have no reason to. Why shouldn't we remember it and hold fast? We have every reason to do so!

'You shall remember the *Lord, your* God!' We are not asked to remember God in general. We are in constant temptation to think of some abstraction when we pronounce or hear the word 'God'. We think of the highest, the deepest, the absolute, the ultimate. But this highest and perhaps ultimate force might be merely fate's powerful coercion and manipulation. So, too, it might be some majestic mystery reigning way above the stars or dwelling in our own hearts. So, too, it might be a purely human invention. To believe that this 'God', this abstract God, gives us power is likely to be a thoroughly uncertain business. Where would he get it from? How could he be the Lord? How could he be your God? Yes, even if he were your God, the result might be terrible, for this 'God' might well turn out to be a malicious Lord, the worst enemy of yourself and of us all.

The *Lord, your* God is a God with a name, a face, a personality. His name, face and personality assure us that he is indeed stern, yet good and faithful, a God whom we used to call as children, and still may call today, a 'dear' God. He is a God who can dispense with, and dispenses us from, the human attempt to form an opinion or elaborate a theory about him. He is indeed the God who has told us long ago and tells us time and again how and what *we shall think of him*. Strangely enough, he does so by revealing what *he thinks of us*. He might well have be-littling and disparaging thoughts about us. Yet these are barred from his mind. He thinks indeed very highly of us! Because we are such excellent people? No, even though we are not excellent at all! Perhaps because he is in need of us? No, he does not need us. He could quite easily do without us. He thinks so highly of us because he is deeply moved by our need of him, our bitter, inescapable need. Is his perhaps the casualness and condescension of a great ruler, occasionally bending down to the man in the street? Not in the least. He takes our place and surrenders himself for us, thereby binding himself to us and compromising himself with us once for all. He is the God of Christmas of whom we sing:

> A tiny child and poor he came
> To give us mercy's blessing.

This is the height and the depth, the ultimate and eternal power and glory of the almighty *Lord*: he has mercy on us. Having mercy on you and on me, he is *your* God and *my* God. Because he is compassionate, it is not particularly difficult, but the most natural thing in the world to believe in him, to hope for him and to love him, and to love our neighbour accordingly. It is he, *this* God who gives you power.

He gives you power! Power is know-how, skill, freedom to do something. It is our human predicament that we should know how to do so many things we can't do, that we need so much power and strength we don't have. We need strength to live, and we need even more strength to die. I am not thinking so much at this point of what will happen to us at the end of our days as of the failures and defaults of all human life, from its very beginnings. We need strength to be young, and we need even more strength to grow up and to grow old.

We need strength not to grow bitter and not to despair in the disappointments of life and in times of bad luck. We need even more strength not to become wanton, vain and foolish when things go well and good luck is with us. We need strength to withstand the temptations all too well known to us, and we may need even greater strength not to become self-sufficient, loveless pharisees when we do withstand them. We certainly need strength to be imprisoned as you are in this house but, believe me, we may even need more strength to be free and to make good use of our freedom. We need strength to get along with our fellowmen who may get on our nerves and annoy us, and perhaps we need greater strength to get along with ourselves, to live in peace with ourselves day by day and year by year. Yes, we need many and manifold kinds of strength, all effective and unfailing, yet we lack them. We cannot provide strength ourselves. Nor can anybody else give it to us. The urgent exhortation: 'You must, you ought to!' is in vain. What we need is the strength only he can give who is the source of all power and strength. He does not want to keep it for himself, but wants to give it to us and indeed does give it to us.

I am certainly in no position to describe how this happens. How could God's giving of his own, of what is his, be described? One thing is certain: he gives us the power and strength we need in our human weakness, yours and mine, precisely when we are at our wit's end. When it happens, it will always be an unexpected event. God always gives us strength for one leg of the journey at a time. At each stage we are promised that he will continue to provide additional and greater strength as needed on our way into the future. The powers we receive each time somehow enable us to do the very things we had been incapable of doing so far. God does not distribute the full ration all at once. He apportions it from one day to the next. You will not be a rock of strength overnight. Neither will you remain a weakling, worth nothing but writhing, throwing up your hands in despair and falling on your face (that will happen often enough!). God gives you strength and power to become a man, modestly yet determinedly, who goes his way, humbly yet courageously, and is strong and grateful: strong because it is God's almighty grace for which he is grateful.

The Lord your God does all these things, he gives you the strength and power you need and lack, as surely as he has compassion on us, as surely as he has already cared for us in the manger of Bethlehem and on the cross of Golgotha, as surely as in Jesus Christ we are his children whom he never forgets or tires of remembering.

Therefore, you too, *remember* the Lord your God! My dear friends, we all are peculiar customers of God—myself included even before all others, as I readily admit. We are people who time and again are blind to the fact that it is he who gives us power, who time and again are careless and not in the least grateful, who are reluctant to receive with empty, outstretched hands what he gives, what he alone possesses and alone is able and willing to give: the power and strength we need yet lack so desperately. Yes, we are these peculiar customers of our God. This confession, however, must not be our last word.

Remember the Lord, your God! This means: awake from the sleep of your great thoughtlessness! Awake from the happy or unhappy dreams and the countless thoughts that wander through your mind! Awake to the insight and knowledge that it is he who gives you power! If you do awake, the question will inevitably occur to you: 'How on earth could I forget him? How could I consider everything else more important than him? How could I push myself so much to the centre of things? How could I measure all and everything according to my desires and values? As if I were the Greenwich Observatory with its meridian dividing East and West? How could I, really?' But then don't waste time. Quickly drive this one nail into the wall: 'It is he!'

and quickly hang everything on it. He is the number 'one' before all the zeros, the one behind which all these zeros may alone mean anything. He measures according to his unfailing rule. He judges justly. Above all, he and he alone gives what we need. He possesses it. He is its very source. He will not keep it from us. To remember *this* is to *remember* the Lord!

I am sure that if you do this, if you remember the Lord your God, the power he gives you—like the water from the rock touched by Moses' rod—begins to trickle, to flow, to rush into your heart and into your life, carrying with it comfort, joy and peace for this coming year and all the following years, power to you, precisely to you!

You might ask me now whether and how we can remember the Lord. Two answers to these questions by way of conclusion.

Remembering the Lord, like all good things, must be begun, repeated and practised. You ask me how to begin, how to repeat, how to practise this remembrance? In reply I point to the Christian community, even as it exists in this house. I was once asked here in a discussion what the 'Church' really was. I might now give the plainest answer. The Church is our common attempt to remember our God. We remember the Lord when we preach and hear the sermon. We remember the Lord when, as we did at Christmas, we celebrate the Lord's Supper, where it becomes tangible, so to speak, that it is he who feeds and nourishes us and gives us strength. We remember the Lord when we sing (with understanding!) the hymns of our hymnals and when we read the Bible, as indeed we may and we must do, perhaps the 90th Psalm beginning with these words: 'Lord, thou hast been our dwelling place in all generations.' Or the 103rd Psalm: 'Bless the Lord, O my soul, and all that is within me, bless his holy name! Bless the Lord, O my soul, and forget not all his benefits!' Or the wonderful 23rd Psalm: 'The Lord is my shepherd, I shall not want!' But I would have to quote the whole Bible which tells me on each page that 'it is he who gives you power!' Have you seriously tried all these things? And will you then seriously say: 'I cannot remember the Lord, my God?'

However—and this is my second answer—even in worship, even during the sermon, even with hymnal and Bible in hand, it does not happen at will that we are able to remember the Lord. Nothing will come of it unless he himself gives us power to remember him. Over and above all we might contribute ourselves, we must pray that he grants us this power. We certainly may pray for it. And with great confidence I assure you that you may not only believe, you may also *know* that this is true—the Lord our God has never failed anyone who prayed for power and strength to remember him. Amen.

Dear Father in Jesus Christ, thy Son, our brother and Lord! Thou hast brought us together here. Abide with us, we beseech thee, and accompany each one of us to his own place when we depart. Do not abandon anyone! Do not let anyone completely lose himself! Above all, forbid that anyone of us forget thee, not remember thee! Lighten, comfort and strengthen also our loved ones near and far, our friends and even more our foes!

Before thee we would lay the known and unknown sorrows, needs and necessities of all people; those of the Christian Church at home and abroad; those of the men and women called to debate, advise, govern and decide the destinies of East and West; those of the humiliated and exploited here and there, of the poor, the sick and the old, of all the embittered, the disheartened and the perplexed, of the whole world longing for justice, freedom and peace. Let many, let all, and thus let us experience that we are in the hands of thy almighty grace, which will ultimately bring an end to all injustice and misery and create a new heaven and a new earth where righteousness shall dwell!

Glory be to thee, Father, Son and Holy Ghost, who wast and art and art to come, now and for evermore. Amen.

TEACH US TO NUMBER OUR DAYS

16 March 1958

O Lord, our God and our Father! We thank thee for the privilege
of calling on thee and listening to thee together. Before thee
we are all equal. Thou knowest the life, the thoughts, the ways and
the hearts of each one of us, even our innermost secrets. No one is
righteous in thy sight, not one. Yet thou hast not forgotten nor rejected
nor condemned a single one among us. Rather, thou lovest each one of
us. Thou knowest our needs and art ever willing to satisfy them.
Thou lookest only upon the empty, outstretched hands which thou
desirest to fill to overflowing. In the suffering and death of Jesus,
thy dear Son, thou hast taken our place, mercifully beyond compre-
hension. Thou hast made our darkness and our misery thine own and
hast set us free to walk in thy light as thy children, and to be joyful.

In Christ's name, we beseech thee, pour some portion of thy Holy
Spirit upon each and every one of us, that we may understand thee,
as well as ourselves and each other, a little better in this hour. Quickened
and encouraged by thy Holy Spirit—whether we acknowledge it yet
or not—may we advance on the path which thou hast traced for us
in all eternity when Jesus on the cross bowed his head and died. Amen.

DEAR BROTHERS AND SISTERS, today let us turn to a portion of Scripture which may sound familiar to many of you since it is often quoted at funeral services. It is the 12th verse of the 90th Psalm: *So teach us to number our days that we may get a heart of wisdom.* This is the way the modern Zurich Bible, and most English translations render this verse. Luther, however, translated 'Teach us to remember that we must die, that we may become wise.' You know that the Old Testament was originally written in Hebrew. This raises problems of translation. We are entitled to ask which version comes closest to the original. You have no doubt noticed the difference in wording between the two translations. Yet their meaning is the same. He who numbers his days remembers that they are counted. In other words, he remembers that he must die. To become truly wise means to get a heart of wisdom. For, in the biblical language, the heart is the very centre of human life. The quality of the heart settles the question whether the whole person is foolish or wise. What, then, can we learn from this text?

Our days are numbered, we must die. That is quite obviously true. One dies earlier, the other a little later, one perhaps after a long illness, another quite suddenly, one almost imperceptibly, another in agony. No one can escape his death. Holbein once illustrated the human destiny on the walls of the nearby Square, which used to be a cemetery and is called to this day 'Dance-of-Death Square' in remembrance of Holbein's murals. But what is the use of telling us that our days are numbered and we must die? We know it all too well already! There is no need for us to meet here and to open our Bible to get this insight. That man is mortal is somehow part of his natural history.

But, according to Luther's translation, it is important to *remember* this well-known fact. Are we then urged to ponder the common knowledge of our mortal condition? That might indeed be a quite appropriate undertaking. I am reminded of a painting portraying a great Catholic saint who contemplates a skull in his hand. He is obviously meditating on the fact that he must die. Even for us, who are no saints, it might now and again be a thought-provoking experience to walk through a cemetery, to look at the tomb-stones and the crosses in memory of the many, many people who once lived like us and then died, and to get it clear in our minds that one day we shall follow them. But honestly, what is the result if *we* attempt to number our days? Do we really know what it means: *to die*? True, we may know that everything will be over for us one day. But what does it help to reckon with *this*? A very good friend of mine often takes pleasure in posing before me as an unbeliever. He likes to mention his own reflection on human mortality, the result being, he says, that death is nothing but a transition or a return to nature, man falling like a leaf from the tree to the ground and returning to dust. Nothing particularly serious to think about, he feels. Mind you, he is a man who is not entirely without wisdom (he might not be my friend otherwise!). But he certainly did not get it through profound thinking about death.

The message of our text, therefore, lies neither in the quite superfluous statement that we, like all mortal beings, must die, nor in the questionable exhortation that *we* should attempt to remember and ponder this well-known fact. *So teach us to number our days*, the wording goes. *Teach!* This is an invocation, a petition addressed to God. It is a supplication, a prayer. We do not usually ask for something we are able to do or to get by ourselves. But there are things which we are unable to do or to get by ourselves, among them those brought to mind in our text. This is why it begins with '*Teach* us'. 'Give us, grant us, create within us the readiness and the ability to remember that we must die! You, O Lord God, must teach us to number our days, like a teacher teaches the alphabet and the two-plus-two to a little child who cannot know these things by himself. For this teaching we would ask!'

As a petition, the text assumes that the chapter called death in the natural history of human life is after all worth thinking about. It reminds us, moreover, of our inability to summon the right thoughts about death into our hearts and minds, and at the same time of the urgent necessity to ponder the matter nevertheless, lest we fail to become wise, to get a heart of wisdom. Lastly, the text points to the only way out of this dilemma: to cast ourselves upon God, imploring him to give us, to grant us, to teach us to remember that we must die. The word we have heard is a word of prayer, inviting us whenever it is pronounced to join in the petition: 'So teach us to number our days!'

God *hears* and *answers* this petition. Then we can and we may summon the right and relevant thoughts about death. Then God himself teaches us, grants us, gives us the freedom to number our days.

We do not know how the Old Testament writer of the 90th Psalm envisioned God making man free and able to meditate on his mortal condition, much less what the right, the God-given meditation itself is like. We only hear him *petition* in this psalm. Petition is already a great undertaking, even more so when we allow ourselves to be called to do it. It is no exaggeration to say that the Old Testament is essentially one great supplication, particularly, though not exclusively, in regard to death. Without joining in the petition of the Old Testament, we cannot understand the New Testament. Yet one thing is even greater than our human petition. It is God's hearing and answering it, as borne out in the New Testament, most clearly, by the way, again with reference to the subject of death we are talking about. There is a right way to number our days, and God himself has opened it up for us. Without the greater event of the New Testament the already great event of the Old Testament would remain hidden from us. Because the New Testament brings to light how God hears and answers our requests, we are even more urgently called to make the fervent petition our own: 'So teach us to number our days. . . !'

We must go on to consider how God *hears* and *answers* this petition. To begin with, let me state it shortly and boldly: To remember, and to remember aright, that we must die is to remember that *Jesus has died for us*. We may and we must know him in his suffering and death, as we are most vividly reminded to do in the Lenten season we are about to enter. Only then do we come to a true understanding of what our own death is all about, that truly a bit more is involved than a short chapter of our natural history. Here I must add a significant detail to the description I gave you earlier of the old saint. He is indeed shown in the painting not only with a skull in his hand, but facing a cross with the figure of the Crucified. Beyond the skull the saint's eyes are fixed upon the dying Jesus. The artist obviously knew that the right contemplation of our mortal condition is the contemplation of Jesus' death for our sake. Let me try to explain the twofold meaning of this death.

Do you know what this is, the death of Jesus? What happened? What was fulfilled at that moment? A mere necessity of nature? An accident or incident? No, the death of Jesus was a *judgment*. This is the first thing to be said and retained. It is the carrying out of a death sentence, inflicted upon Jesus instead of ourselves. *We* are judged in his person. *We* are condemned and killed in his death. Of course not we ourselves, but someone who has very much to do with us, someone who stands intimately by our side: the old man who dwells and spooks about within us all! This old man in us is judged, sentenced and killed in Jesus' death. He is extinguished from head to toe, including his heart, his mind, his will, his feelings, his low instincts and his high aspirations, his superficiality and his depth, his bestiality and his spirituality, his evil deeds and his good works, his misery and his glory. God has spoken his 'no' to the whole inventory of the old man in us, having no use for him, discarding him, delivering him to death. What Jesus had to bear in our place was nothing less than this hard and irrevocable 'no', spoken by God upon this old man in us. Jesus accepted to die the death of the old man. He suffered this death in his flesh.

And now *our* own death occurs in the power of Jesus' death in our place. Certainly only in *his* power! For no other man will ever again die this death, the death of the One judged in the place of all others. Our death happens in the power of his death, as the consequence, reflection and sign of the divine 'no', of the judgment carried out in Jesus' condemnation. This is our predicament. This is the situation of the old man dwelling and spooking about within us all. He is worthless. He is written off, rejected, nailed to a cross and killed, precisely as it happened to Jesus before the eyes of the whole world.

To number our days, to remember that we must die, means in the first place to let the power of Jesus' death work in us, to acknowledge and endure our predicament. As surely as Jesus took our place when he suffered and was crucified, died and was buried, as surely are we condemned. The wise heart which we covet, which may be our prize, is the *humble* heart, humbled by the power of the death of Jesus. It is the heart of a man who gains an ever astute and lasting knowledge that before God he has nothing to present, nothing to claim and nothing to boast, even if he were the best and most pious of all human beings. The wise heart belongs to a man who knows that in the hour of his death he will have nothing to rely upon except God's mercy, who knows that he cannot live except from God's mercy, who knows that already today this is true. He who knows this has obtained a heart of wisdom. This is the first thing to keep in mind.

But there is another and quite different thing to be remembered. What happened in the death of Jesus did not happen against us, but *for us*. What took place was not an act of God's wrath against man. Quite the opposite holds true. Because in the one Jesus God so loved us from all eternity—truly all of us

—because he has elected himself to be our dear Father and has elected us to become his dear children whom he wants to save and to draw unto him, therefore he has in the one Jesus written off, rejected, nailed to a cross and killed our old man who, as impressively as he may dwell and spook about in us, is not our true self. God so acted for our own sake. In the death of Jesus he has cleared away, swept out and let go up in flames, smoke and ashes the old man in us, that we may live a life of freedom. That he may himself say to us his divine 'yes', valid once for all and unconditionally, he has chosen to say his divine 'no', once for all and unconditionally, to this old companion who has no traffic with our true self, to our old ways and by-ways, and he did say 'no', unmistakably, in the death of Jesus as the substitute for us.

And now *our* own death occurs in the power of the *gracious and saving* death which Jesus suffered for our sake. Only in the power of *his* death, only as a consequence, reflection and sign. For no other man ever suffered or will suffer death that he may mercifully redeem the whole world. In our living and in our dying the power of the saving grace of Jesus' death for us is unfailingly at work.

Hence our life and at the appointed hour our death also may now happen in the power of the great 'yes' spoken to us by God when Jesus died on the cross. Do you know who you really are? Do you know who you will be in your last hour? Because the old man—you know him well enough—has already been extinguished in the death of Jesus, because you may no longer be this old man, because your own case has been disposed of by the power of Jesus' death, therefore you yourself are now the new man, loved by God, chosen, saved and accepted by him who has said to you and will say to you his divine 'yes'. Take courage: this is what you are, for the time being in the bit of time, long or short, which still may lie ahead of you, ultimately in your death, as it will occur in the power of the death of Jesus.

To number our days, to remember that we must die, means therefore in the second place properly to rejoice in the effectiveness of this power, to acknowledge with thankful hearts the true situation of our life and death, and to be nourished by its unspeakable beauty, victory and glory! As surely as Jesus himself, when he suffered and was crucified, died and was buried for us, brought forth our new and eternal life, as surely may we look and walk toward our own death with confidence. This is what we must remember! If God teaches us to number our days, we may approach our death, through the power of Jesus' death, as our life, our eternal life. The heart of wisdom we hope to get is the joyous heart of one who, living or dying, expects everything from *God* alone—indeed from him *everything*. He is one who holds to God's grace alone, indeed is wholly held by it, in the hours, days and years he may yet be allowed to live, and even more when he will depart, because he knows he will die in the power of the death of Jesus.

I am at the end. Must I still explain how God goes about teaching us to number our days? Let me give you the plainest answer: God teaches us by *telling* us and by letting us *hear* of the twofold power, both killing and life-giving, of Jesus' death in our dying.

There can be no doubt: God tells us and he lets us hear. He is not found wanting. He teaches us to number our days. In all the fire of his Holy Spirit he teaches us that we must die, that Jesus has died for us.

My dear brothers and sisters, if only a spark of this fire kindles the heart of a man, whoever he is and whatever his plight, nothing is lost for him! Everything is gained! Amen.

O Lord our God! We come into thy presence with the heartfelt request that thou wilt accept us, granting us no rest until we are willing to rest in thee—that thou wilt fight against us and for us until thy peace reigns in our hearts, our thoughts and conversation, in our very being and in our living together. Without thee we can do nothing; with thee and in thy service we can do all things.

Be present and active in all parts of this house, so also throughout the city, among all its inhabitants and today especially everywhere where thy Church gathers together. Be with the sick and dying, all who are destitute, oppressed or have gone astray, so also with those who rule, who mould public opinion and hold in their hands the means of power, in our country as well as in the large nations! Pour out thy love to oppose rampant hate, thy reason to oppose unreason; oh that from thee might flow not merely a trickle but a torrent of justice to oppose so much injustice! But thou knowest better than us what is best for us and the world—ultimately destined, as it is, for thy glory. So we commend everything into thy hands. So each of us, in his place and in his own way, will calmly, truly and confidently hope in thee.

We call on thee as thy dear Son, our Lord Jesus Christ, has bidden us: 'Our Father . . .'

THE BEGINNING OF WISDOM

20 July 1958

Holy and merciful God! Great is thy lovingkindness, for thou hast given us this day and gathered us here so that we may call upon thee and hear thy word of comfort and admonition.

What are we human beings before thee? How much conceit, hardness of heart and falsehood is there in our thoughts, words and deeds! And as a result, how much confusion and perplexity, how much suffering and misery do we find here and everywhere on this earth!

Yet as we are faced with this predicament, thy fatherly heart is open to us, thy hand remains strong to hold us, to guide us and free us. Thou dost not forget nor reject anyone of us. Thou art near to all of us. Thou dost call us all.

Grant that we may be attentive to thy lovingkindness this Sunday morning! See thou that what we now pray and sing, preach and hear, be not done in vain, but to thy glory and to the awakening, enlightening and lifting up of us all. For Jesus Christ's sake, in whose name we call on thee: 'Our Father . . .'

MY DEAR BROTHERS AND SISTERS, wisdom, our subject this morning, is quite evidently a great thing. Let us be clear about this: it is different from, it is better than, cleverness. Many a man is clever, and yet is not wise. Furthermore, wisdom is greater and better than science which is to be learned in school or from books and speeches. You may believe me, for I come from the University and know a little about scholars. There are men steeped in science who are not wise men at all. Wisdom is also greater and better than cunning. Many a man has proved to be very cunning in a particular situation, but in his lack of wisdom and with all his cunning turned out to be very stupid.

What, then, is wisdom? Wisdom is the knowledge of life or, as we might say, the art of living. Knowledge and art both presuppose ability. This is the greatest knowledge as well as the most difficult art: to be able to live! Not to let one's life drift into illfated disorder, but to give it substance and direction! He who is able to live rightly, is a wise man. But how do we get wisdom, this ability to live?

It is often said that all we need to become wise is to grow old. Don't believe it! I am a rather old man and therefore I know that old age is no guarantee of wisdom. Old age is no shield against folly. It is also said that experience makes a man wise. But heaven knows what experiences we have all had! Did we gain wisdom? Think of the experience of the people of Europe and of the world during the past fifty years! Did they grow wise? Or again, some of you may have heard about psychology. This is the science of man's inner life. Many are convinced that, rightly understood and applied, psychology would lead us to wisdom, to the art of living. I have no intention of speaking against this worthy science. Nevertheless, I cannot in good conscience admit that psychology as such will lead us to wisdom and knowledge of life, particularly when I think of some people I have observed who are very well versed in it. No, 'the fear of the Lord is the beginning of wisdom', we are told. But what is this wisdom, this knowledge of life? What is the connection between wisdom and the fear of the Lord? Let us pursue these questions further.

Let me begin by recalling a story from the Old Testament. The name of King Solomon probably sounds familiar to all of you. There is a story about this king in the third chapter of the first Book of Kings. Solomon, when he was very young, had a dream in the city of Gibeon. None other than the Lord himself is said to have appeared to him, saying: 'Ask what I shall give you.' This sounds like a fairy tale, doesn't it, and yet it was a very serious order. Young Solomon did not answer: 'Give me money, honour, victory over my enemies, give me a long life!' Rather, he replied: 'I shall now be king over this great people of Israel, although I am but a little child and do not know how to go out or come in. Give me an understanding heart to guide me! Teach me to discern between good and evil! Give me insight to grasp what justice is!' These requests so pleased God that he is said to have promised Solomon: 'Behold, I give you a wise and discerning mind, so that none like you has been before and none like you shall arise after you.' When Solomon woke from his dream, he went to Jerusalem, brought God a burnt offering and made a great feast for all his servants. This is the story of Solomon, how he became the wise Solomon, the one who knew the art of living. What may we learn from this story?

Solomon became wise—he proved himself wise already—in that *he did not presume to be wise*, as do so many young people, and even older and old ones. He was not ashamed to confess: 'I am but a little child and do not know how to go out or come in', and therefore he begged God: 'Give me wisdom!' He who does not acknowledge and confess to be such a child, to be very childish indeed, he who presumes to have grasped, understood and discerned wisdom, is most certainly not wise. 'Claiming to be wise, they become fools'. He is wise, whether young or old, who knows he is a child not knowing how to go out or come in. He is wise who sings with the little children: *Ich kann allein nicht gehen, nicht einen Schritt* ('I cannot take one step alone', a line from a well-known German children's hymn). Wisdom has this characteristic: nobody has it stored away; nobody is *already* wise, not in his mind, and even less in his heart. We may only *become* wise. All may, and all should, gain wisdom, and yet all may and should gain it only as people who ask for it with empty hands outstretched. The fear of the Lord is needed to make this beginning in the art of living. He who does not fear the Lord betrays himself by his insistence that he needs no counsel because he is his own counsel. If only others will let him alone to go his own way! Thus does a man think and talk who does not fear the Lord. He who fears him stretches out his hands, asking for discernment and understanding, for wisdom and thereby for the art of living which he does not yet possess. He is ready to receive, to accept the gift.

Solomon became wise, and was wise, in that he asked for things he needed *not for himself, but for others*. To be king was his lot, to reign was his duty, and all his thoughts were centred on this task. He understood his life as a service to be rendered not for his own good, but for the good of his people, the people of God. His one and only problem was how to serve faithfully, how to become a good king, how to avoid becoming a fifth wheel, or a parasite, or like one of those handsome dummies displaying clothes in a shop window. His great problem was how to be a man in the full sense of the word, responsible among, with and for his fellowmen, willing and prepared to act in their behalf. Solomon was a man who understood that only as a true fellow-man could he become a true man. He also understood that he was in need of an understanding and a wise heart in order to be a fellowman to his fellowmen. Most importantly, he understood that he lacked such a heart and could only be given one. This is what he asked for. And this is why he became and was wise. This is wisdom! The fear of the Lord is needed to make such a beginning. He who does not fear the Lord, he who is not wise, will think and speak differently. He will ask: 'What do I need for myself? How do I make a living? What is pleasant in my eyes? What is fun for me?' Conversely, he who fears the Lord constantly hears the commandment: 'Thou shalt love thy God with all thy heart, and thy neighbour as thyself.' He will find himself placed at the service of this neighbour, and will ask himself: 'How can I serve him best?'

Solomon became wise, and was wise, in that he asked for the *ability to discern between good and evil*—between that which is above and that which is below, between what comes first and what comes next, between what may and must by all means happen and what may and must not happen by any means. It is not at all self-evident that man has a capacity for this kind of discernment. It is not innate. Yet this capacity to discern is essential if man is to live his life in the service of others. How could he serve them without this gift? He would only cause disaster around him! This is why the godfearing man will again and again stretch out his empty hands. This is why he can only ask. Solomon was wise because he asked God precisely for this capacity to discern between good and evil. But even this beginning of wisdom, even this insight (This is what is important! This is what I need!) presupposes the fear of the Lord. He who does not fear the Lord will again act quite differently. Either he will not bother discerning at all and, constantly confusing good and evil, will wobble like a drunkard on his way. Or he will be only too sure of himself, of his opinions regarding good and evil, and will march along his way as stiff as a board, a true Pharisee, dealing out judgment and condemnation to the right and to the left as he pleases. Both possibilities are equally grim! He who fears the Lord will most earnestly want to be able to discern between good and evil, but he will want to learn it from God himself. He will turn to God to be taught.

Solomon became wise, and was wise, in that he wished for one thing, and one thing only: *an understanding heart for his service.* Wisdom brings with it integration of all human faculties, singlemindedness and concentration of the one thing necessary. All the rest, all the things that seem good, wholesome fun to man, and maybe are, will be included and in a certain sense hidden in this one thing. We heard how Solomon did not get shortchanged, how, on the contrary, he even received things he had not asked for. He received them because he had not asked for them! Unconcerned, he had asked for one thing only, for the understanding heart and the discerning mind, which was needed for his service as a king. This was his wisdom. But it takes the fear of the Lord to make such a beginning in wisdom, in the art of living. How could he who does not fear the Lord know that one thing, and one thing only, is necessary? How could he possibly avoid the idea that what is needed is his restless craving and piling up of whatever he can get lest he end up shortchanged? He who fears the Lord does not seek after many things, but singlemindedly seeks after the one thing that is necessary, quite content that he will receive all the rest with it.

But what actually is this 'fear of the Lord'? A wrong kind of fear abounds around us, and is not to be confused with the right fear of the Lord. It would be better to call it *anxiety.* We are afraid of bad and dangerous people, afraid of spooks, afraid of death, afraid of the atom bomb, afraid of the Russians and especially afraid of ourselves, because we do not know how to go out and to come in and refuse to admit it! All this fear, this anxiety, is not the beginning, but the end of wisdom. Such fears have nothing, really nothing in common with the fear of the Lord. They have nothing to do with God, the true Lord, but only with little, apparent lords. In the face of all these fears we may and we must cling to the word of the gospel not to be anxious. Wisdom that springs from the fear of the Lord is the end of all these fears.

Moreover, there exists a false, a merely apparent, fear of the Lord, which is even less to be confused with the right fear of the Lord. *Anxiety* would again be a better name for it. We are afraid of God because he is so great and mighty, and we are so small and weak. We are afraid that he will accuse us like an oversized giant prosecutor, and that he will judge us like some sky-scraping chief justice. We may also be afraid of God because he might send us for ever to hell at the end of our days. All such fear has nothing in common with the fear of the Lord. When I was a small boy I had a wellmeaning but somewhat foolish Sunday School teacher who thought it right to provide us children with a precise description of hell and of the eternal punishment awaiting evil people. We were of course immensely interested and likewise excited. But surely not one of us children learned the fear of the Lord and the beginning of wisdom from this. Such reflection about God will almost certainly end up in fleeing, through some kind of a backdoor, to the wrong assurance that things cannot be so bad after all. In the face of this false fear of God we may again be comforted by the gospel word: be not anxious. And wisdom is surely the end of all such false fear of God.

What, then, is the right fear of the Lord?

Let me go back to the 111th Psalm. It is worth noting that this psalm which ends with the fear of the Lord begins with these words: *Praise the Lord, I will give thanks to the Lord with my whole heart.* And it continues: *He has caused his wonderful works to be remembered; the Lord is gracious and merciful. He provides food for those who fear him: he is ever mindful of his covenant.* And later: *The works of his hands are faithful and just; all his precepts are trustworthy.* And immediately before our text: *He sent redemption to his people; he has commanded his covenant for ever.* This leads to the passage on the fear of the Lord. This is the fear of the Lord: it is born, it is given as soon as man discovers that God is *this* God and does *these* things of which the psalm speaks.

It is nothing short of a discovery when a man is suddenly confronted with this reality. It is not unlike the experience of Columbus who, sailing out for India, suddenly hit upon the continent of America. *This* I did not know. *This* nobody ever told me. *This* I could never have found out by myself—that God is *this* God, that God does *these* things. Solomon faced this fact, this lovingkindness, these mighty deeds which God accomplished with his people, with his father, David and with himself. And faced with this wondrous reality, he feared the Lord. Out of this fear he became the wise Solomon.

When the right fear of the Lord takes possession of our hearts, we are both lost in amazement and struck by awe, even terror. For we discover that God, since the beginning of time, has not hated or threatened you and me, but has loved and chosen us, has made a covenant with us, has been our helper long before we knew it and will continue this relationship. The fear of the Lord springs from the discovery that the high and eternal God gave his beloved son for us, for you and me, taking upon himself our sin and our misery; he made his son, our Lord Jesus Christ, to be our brother, for whose sake we may call God our Father and ourselves his children. The fear of the Lord springs from the discovery that I did not merit this gift, that it has been given to me by the pure and free goodness of God, in spite of all I deserved. The fear of the Lord springs from the discovery that this is the true relationship between God and me—that I had totally ignored it—that I had perhaps heard it once from afar, only to forget it again and to live as if it were not true and none of my concern. The fear of the Lord springs from the discovery that it might be high time to awake from sleep, to arise and live as the men we really are, God's elect and chosen people, brothers and sisters of Jesus Christ, set free by him from our sin and our misery. The fear of the Lord springs from the discovery that God calls us unto himself and that his calling urges us to wake up, to arise, and to begin to live as his children. This fear of the Lord is very real, it is awe, even terror, yet is poles apart from the dumb anxiety of which we spoke. For it is inspired with secret jubilation and is born of gratitude.

This fear of the Lord is the beginning of wisdom, the beginning with which we are all called to begin. Each one of us, even the most evil or most foolish person may quite simply begin here, today, tomorrow, every day, and may become versed in the knowledge of living (I almost said 'an artist in living' or even a modest Solomon). Our text continues, *A good understanding have all those who practise it*, and closes with these words: *His praise endures for ever!* Already in this life the wise man lives beyond death. Already here and now he may begin to live eternally.

And now there remains only one question, dear brothers and sisters. I must ask each one of you: 'Have you also made the discovery which leads quite inevitably to the fear of the Lord as the beginning of wisdom?' What would be your answer? This much is certain: there is not a single person here present who cannot and may not make this discovery, no one who may not experience this fear of the Lord, no one to whom it may not become the beginning of wisdom and therefore no one who may be denied living in time for eternity. Rely on this: *No one!* As surely as Jesus Christ has died and risen for us all! Amen.

O Lord our God, our dear Father in Jesus Christ! Yes, what we have preached and heard can and may become evident and acceptable to all of us right here and now. But only thou canst bring this about. And we ask thee to do that, to let us discover who thou art and what thou dost, to awaken in us the fear of thee which springs from thankfulness, to let this fear become for us the beginning of wisdom, so that we may lift our heads and live. Only thou canst give this. Give it then to us, our faithful God!

We ask thee also in thy great and infinite mercy to care for all the people in this house and for their loved ones, for all those in distress, doubt or temptation, for all the sick, the poor and the mentally ill, for all the lonely and the abandoned. We ask thee for those in this town and in this country who govern, judge, teach, write newspapers, for the mighty rulers and their people in the East and in the West, that they shrink from the brink of war and work for peace. We pray especially for the Christian Churches here and and in every corner of the earth, for our Evangelical brethren as well as for the Roman Catholic Church and all other Christian communities, that they may all faithfully and joyfully serve thee and thy word and thereby their fellowmen.

Lord, what would happen to us without thee? What would happen to all that we human beings here and everywhere attempt and do in so much weakness and wickedness? In thee alone do we trust. Lord, have mercy upon us! Amen

HE STANDS BY US

Before a Christmas Communion, 1958

O Lord, our God! Thou hast chosen to dwell not only in heaven on high, but also down on earth with us; not only to be exalted and mighty, but lowly and poor like us; not only to reign, but also to serve us; not only to remain the eternal God, but to be born, to live and to die as a man for our salvation.

In thy dear Son, our Saviour Jesus Christ, thou hast given us no less than thyself so that we may belong to thee once and for all. This gift is offered to us all, even though not one of us deserves it. What else can we do but rejoice in wonder, be thankful, and build on what thou hast done for us?

Grant, we beseech thee, that this may come true among us and in us all. Let us become a true Christmas congregation, as we sincerely and willingly pray and sing, preach and listen. Let us become a true congregation of the Lord's Supper, as we hunger for his communion.

'Our Father . . .'

And she gave birth to her first-born son and wrapped him in swaddling cloths, and laid him in a manger, because there was no place for them in the inn.   LUKE 2.7

MY DEAR BROTHERS AND SISTERS, let me get to the main point without delay. Who is he who was born the son of Mary, wrapped in swaddling cloths, and laid in a manger? Who *is* he? I do not ask who he *was*. Christmas is not the birthday celebration of a man who lived long ago, then died and passed away, and whose centennial we solemnly commemorate. True, he once lived and then died—and *how* he died!—but he also rose from the dead; he lives and is present among us now, much closer to each one of us than we are to ourselves. Still, who is he? The answer to this question is the good news of Christmas.

Today let me say simply this: *He who was born in the stable is he who stands by you, stands by me and stands by us all.* I do not say *one* who stands by you, but *he* who stands by you. For only One, only he who was born on the first Christmas Day, can stand by us in utter unselfishness and with ultimate authority and power.

I would like to state it in very personal terms. *He stands by you —and by you—and by you!* When I point my finger at you, each one must know he is personally addressed. Yes, he stands by *you*! This is what you yearn for, this is what you desire. You cannot live without a fellow human being. You may ask now: 'Who is he who really wants to stand by me? And a further question will immediately rise in your mind: Is there some one, or perhaps is there no one who is willing and able to stand by me? Perhaps nobody cares? Do all others pass me by like the priest and the Levite in the parable of the good Samaritan? Or have they even turned against me?' When such questions beset you, a great loneliness may have descended upon you, and you felt totally deserted. And then you came very close to saying: 'If no one is ready to stand by me, I shall stand by myself!' But this is a great, even the very greatest error! A drowning man cannot pull himself out of the water by his own hair. Neither can you do it. Someone else must rescue you.

This is the good news of Christmas. He who stands by you and helps you is alive and present! It is he who was born that Christmas Day! Open your eyes, open your ears, open your heart! You may truly see, hear and experience that he is here, and stands by you as no one else can do! He stands by you, really by you, now and for evermore!

He stands by you without ulterior motive, without thinking of himself. Perhaps you asked yourself a while ago: 'Is it really so bad? Does not one or the other of my fellowmen stand by me?' This is quite possible. Yet does there not remain a shadow between him and you, even though he be your very best friend? Perhaps he stands by you as long as he enjoys your company, perhaps expecting that you will reciprocate, perhaps because it makes him feel good. You sense that fundamentally he thinks first of himself; he does not stand by you; he stands only by himself. When this recognition dawns on you, loneliness will again descend on you, only more poignantly.

But, now, the good news of Christmas. He who was born on Christmas Day stands by you, without thinking of himself for one moment. He does not demand anything from you; he demands *you*.

> Love caused thine incarnation,
> Love brought thee down to me;
> Thy thirst for my salvation
> Procured my liberty.
> O love beyond all telling
> That led thee to embrace
> In love, all love excelling,
> Our lost and fallen race.

He is the one who was born that Christmas morning and became your fellowman *par excellence*, your neighbour, your friend, your brother. He reaps no benefit from it. He is not concerned with himself. He is concerned only with you.

He stands by you in the fullness of his authority and power. Suppose you do find a fellowman who stands by you in all adversities. But he will never be more than a man, endowed with only human power. He would certainly like to help you, and he does help you to a certain extent. Yet is it not true that a fellowman can only be of little help and ultimately of no help at all? Let us choose an obvious example. Here you sit, and here I stand before you. I sincerely desire to stand by you. You possibly feel it and even believe me. I might succeed in comforting you and cheering you up by telling you about Christmas. But let us be honest. I cannot help you effectively. I cannot put your life in order. I cannot save you. No man can do this for his fellowmen. No one can stand by the others with unlimited authority and power.

But now, the good news of Christmas! He who was born on Christmas Day is not only the son of Mary; he is also the son of God. If he stands by you, he does so in full power, in the power to help you at any cost, to shield you against each and everyone, above all against your worst enemy, yourself. He stands by you in the power to help you effectively, to carry you, to save you. He is not content to bring you some comfort and good cheer; he is all out to bring you everlasting joy. Only he can bring it, but he really brings it. He stands by you in the power to guide you through this life, and to carry you through death to life eternal. It is he who was born on Christmas Day, your Saviour and mine, the Saviour of us all, the first son of Mary, the first-born of all creation, as it is affirmed elsewhere in the Bible. He, 'Christ the Saviour is born'.

But this is not the whole story. We are furthermore told that there was no room in the inn for Joseph and Mary. No room for him who was to be born and who was born. No room for him who stands by us men in unlimited power and utter selfishness. For him there was no room in the inn.

The inn must have been something like a modest or more fashionable hotel, a nice or not so nice house with guest-rooms, dining-room and lounges. Today it would also include a large garage! It was certainly a comfortable place to stay and to rest and to eat. In this nice and comfortable inn there happened to be no room for the child about to be born, no room for this new guest. There were too many other and better clients around. Too bad! Too bad indeed for this inn! Now Jesus Christ could not be born there. Now he had to be born in totally different surroundings.

What does this say to our situation? The Saviour does not need to be born again. He was born once for all. But he would like to take up quarters among us, by whom he stands so faithfully and so powerfully, whose Saviour he is. What about our various inns? The City Hall, the Casino, the University or the Cathedral could very well be these inns. So could the many private homes and apartments, the restaurants and the stores of Basel. So could the Bundeshaus in Berne, or the Kremlin in Moscow, or the Vatican in Rome, or the White House in Washington. These are inns where he surely would like to dwell. Why not? All these places, including ours here with its work rooms and cells, are inhabited by people. And people are his main concern. By them and by us all he stands, faithfully and powerfully.

But what if in these inns there is no room left? Because there may be people with better status, better jobs and better knowledge who have no place for him? Who have no idea that he who wants to enter is the one who stands by them and whom they so desperately need? What if the doors of all these inns remain closed to him, and everything continues in its old beaten path, since he cannot put up quarters among us? Perhaps this holds also for this house or this cell where you dwell? What if he then went on to other places and other people, far away, possibly to Africa or Asia? I am reminded this moment of a dear friend in Japan who was baptized a few weeks ago after having weighed this step for twenty-five years. Now he has come forward and others do the same, far away from here. What if Christ had already passed by our closed inns? What, then, shall we say?

No doubt a Christmas message is also addressed to the inns and their inhabitants. 'Behold, I stand at the door and knock; if any one hears my voice and opens the door, I will come in to him and eat with him, and he with me.' Yes, *if*. . . ! The good news of Christmas raises indeed a serious question in relation to our various inns.

But I do not want to conclude by raising this question. Fortunately, our story makes one more point. The Saviour did not find room in the inn. But this did not hinder him from being born elsewhere, and in what surroundings! We hear about a manger. We probably find ourselves in a stable or an open-air feeding spot for animals. Certainly not in a nice and comfortable place where people like to dwell because it looks so cosy and homely, or at least decent. No, it was a place compared to which the cells of this house might well be called luxurious. There were animals right beside, oxen and donkeys, as many painters have represented it. In this gloomy place Jesus Christ was born. Likewise, he died in an even gloomier place. There, in the manger, in the stable next to the animals, it happened that the sky opened above the dark earth, that God became man, to be wholly with us and for us. There it happened that this fellowman, this neighbour, this friend, this brother was given to us. There it happened. Thanks be to God, the parents and the baby for whom there was no room in the inn found this other spot where this could happen, and indeed did happen.

And, thanks be to God, as we now consider the Saviour's coming into our own midst, there are not only the various inns where he stands outside, knocking and asking. There is quite another place where he simply enters, indeed has already secretly entered, and waits until we gladly recognize his presence. What kind of a place in our life is this? Do not suggest some presumably noble, beautiful or at least decent compartment of your life and work, where you could give the Saviour a respectable reception. Not so, my friends! The place where the Saviour enters in looks rather like the stable of Bethlehem. It is not beautiful, but quite ugly; not at all cosy, but really frightening; not at all decently human, but right beside the animals. You see, the proud or modest inns, and our behaviour as their inhabitants, are but the surface of our lives. Beneath there lurks the depth, even the abyss. Down below, we are, without exception, but each in his own way, only poor beggars, lost sinners, moaning creatures on the threshold of death, only people who have lost their way.

Down there Jesus Christ sets up quarters. Even better, he has already done so! Yes, praise be to God for this dark place, for this manger, for this stable in our lives! There we need him, and there he can use each one of us. There we are ready for him. There he only waits that we see him, recognize him, believe in him, and love him. There he greets us. What else can we do but return his greeting and bid him welcome? Let us not be ashamed that the oxen and donkeys are close by. Precisely there he firmly stands by us all. In this dark place he will have Holy Communion with us. This is what we now shall have with him and with one another. Amen.

O Lord our God! When we are afraid, abandon us not to despair! When we are disappointed, let us not grow bitter! When we fall, leave us not lying there! When we are at our wit's end and run out of strength, let us not perish! Grant us then the sense of your nearness and your love which thou hast promised to those with a humble and contrite heart who fear thy word. Thy dear Son has come to all men in despair. To overcome our plight he was born in the stable and died on the cross. Awaken us all, O Lord, and keep us awake to acknowledge and confess him!

We remember before thee all darkness and suffering of our time; the manifold errors and misunderstandings whereby we human beings afflict one another; the harsh reality which so many must face without the benefit of comfort; the great dangers that hang over the world which does not know how to counter them. We remember the sick and the mentally ill, the needy, the refugees, the oppressed and the exploited, the children who have no good parents or no parents at all. We remember all those who are called on to help as much as men can help, the officials of our country and of all other countries, the judges and civil servants, the teachers and educators, the writers of books and newspapers, the doctors and nurses in the hospitals, the preachers of thy word in the various churches and congregations nearby and afar. We remember them all when we implore thee to let thy light of Christmas shine brightly, much more brightly than ever, for them and for us, so that they and we ourselves may be helped. We ask all this in the name of the Saviour in whom thou hast already hearkened to our supplications and wilt do so again and again. Amen.

DEATH—BUT LIFE!

Easter Sunday 1959

O Lord our God! We give thee thanks that we, too, may cele- brate Easter together. We give thee thanks because thou art such an unconceivably great, holy and merciful God. When we re- jected, condemned and killed thy dear Son, it was truly thy work, designed to bring about peace in him for us all and for the world. Thou hast then raised him from death and the tomb, as an eternal testimony that thou, the Maker and Lord of all creation, art not against but for us foolish, evil and afflicted men. We give thanks that we, the undeserving, today may preach and hear this word.

And now be thou in our midst! Grant that thy word be rightly preached and rightly heard here! Lead us to thee and to one another that as of one mind we may freely and openly love thee as thou hast loved us, lovest us, and wilt love us, that we may wake up and remain vigilant in humble obedience and joyful hope.

For this we ask in the name of Jesus Christ who commanded us to pray, 'Our Father . . .'

For the wages of sin is death, but the free gift of God is eternal life in Christ Jesus our Lord.   ROMANS 6.23

MY DEAR BROTHERS AND SISTERS, did you hear it? *Death —but life!* When in these days we wish each other 'Good Easter' or 'Happy Easter', we will want to remember that a great deal is at stake: death—but life. These two powerful words meet head-on elsewhere in the Bible. For instance in the Second Letter to Timothy (1.10) it is affirmed, 'Our Saviour Jesus Christ abolished death and brought life and immortality to light through the gospel'. Or in the Gospel according to Saint John (5.24), 'He who hears my word and believes him who sent me ... has passed from death to life'. Lastly, in the First Letter of John we find the following confession by the congregation (3.14): 'We know that we have passed out of death into life'. And now in our text, a word of the apostle Paul, *The wages of sin is death, but the free gift of God is eternal life in Christ Jesus our Lord.*

Let us underline the '*but*'! Death and life are not just two words, concepts, or ideas. They describe a journey, a history embodied in our Lord Jesus Christ on Easter morning when he rose from the dead. Then and there, in him, it was accomplished once for all, but then and there also for us. Hence his Easter story is our history as well. *Death—but life, eternal life!* This is why 'we know that we have passed out of death into life'.

Let us further note the *sequence*. The text does not say 'life, but then death!' It does not say 'out of life into death'. True enough, this would certainly be the itinerary of our own making. First to be young, then grow up, and finally grow old. First to be a little happy and often unhappy, to do some good and even more evil, and finally die and rot in a cemetery or be dispersed into the air in a crematorium. This is our itinerary. God's itinerary, however, is totally different. Death and the tomb marked the beginning of the Easter story. Then followed the 'but'!

Then came the order 'onward', along a one-way street, where no about-turns were possible, into life, life eternal.

> The strife is o'er, the battle done.
> The victory of Life is won.
> The song of triumph hath begun.
>   Alleluya!

This is what happened in the Easter story, in Jesus Christ. Now let us ponder the various moments of this event one by one.

The wages of sin is death. There seems to be no choice but to begin with this beginning of the Easter story.

Death is called here '*the wages of* sin'. It could also be called the pay, the salary, the compensation paid by sin to those who are in its service and work for it. Strange, isn't it? Sin fulfills here the function of the paymaster in the armed services, or of the employer or his cashier in a business enterprise who pays the employees and workers. Here is what is your due, what you have earned through your efforts. Is it the correct amount? Take a good look! Absolutely correct, isn't it? This is what you deserve, and you've got it: death, not more, not less, and nothing else.

But what kind of paymaster or employer is this sin with such a tremendous pay-off? We may all be inclined to think of man's countless foolish and selfish intentions, his twisted and mischievous words and deeds. From all these sin can be known, as a tree can be known from its fruits. Yet these outward signs are not sin itself, the wages of which are death. Sin is not confined to the evil things we *do*. It is the evil within us, the evil which we *are*. Shall we call it our pride or our laziness, or shall we call it the deceit of our life? Let us call it for once the great defiance which turns us again and again into the enemies of God and of our fellowmen, even of our own selves. This defiance in us all is the sin, the lord and master we serve, for whom we toil and by whom we are paid in return with death. This is the only reward this lord and master can offer; it is the only one we deserve. And he will most certainly not withhold it from us, not even over our opposition.

What is *death*, the wages paid by sin? Here again we must think beyond the first caption that may come to mind when we hear the word 'death'. Not only shall we die one day. Death is much greater and much more dangerous than that. It is the great 'no', the shadow that hangs over our human life and accompanies all its movements. It is the judgment which reads: 'You, your life or what you think is life has no meaning because it has no right to exist and therefore cannot last! Your life is a rejected life! It has no value before God or before your fellow-being, not even before yourself!' Death means that this 'no' has been pronounced over us. Death means that we inescapably wither and wilt, returning to dust and ashes. This is death as paid by sin. This 'no', this judgment, is the sum total of our paypacket. When we shall die at the appointed hour, the truth will be disclosed: the wages of sin is death.

This is truly *our* history. One might also say that the history of the world is but one great demonstration of the fact that the wages of sin is death. But let us shelve for a moment the history of the world. It is anyhow best understood when it is seen through the history of our own lives. And here it is crystal-clear; the wages of sin is death. But now mark this! Because Jesus Christ was willing to make *our* history his own; because he took our sin upon himself as though he himself had committed it; because he volunteered in our behalf to pocket the wages of sin —therefore he suffered, was crucified, died and was buried; therefore the Easter story begins with Jesus Christ lying dead in the tomb. This he willed and this he did. All of us lay there. The wages of *our* sin were paid on Easter morning. *Our* death occurred on the cross. The 'no', meant to strike us mightily, struck the one who was without sin and did not deserve death. It was executed in his flesh to the bitter end.

But the free gift of God is eternal life. We have been talking about the dismal beginning of the Easter story. Here is now its glorious outcome; here is the joyous 'onward'; here is the one-way street along which Christ's history proceeded and whereon we, thanks to him, advance too. On this road sin and death, its wages, lie no longer ahead of us, but behind us.

Eternal life was the destination of Christ's journey. It is the destination of our journey as well, since the Easter story happened for us. No backing out, dear brothers and sisters! No return to a life where we once again would labour in the service of sin, of our evil defiance, only to earn and to receive death as the wages of sin! No, forward, into life eternal! Eternal life is man's life when God has spoken his 'yes' upon it, once for all, unconditionally and unreservedly, not to be changed any more. Eternal life is man's life lived with God, in his bright light, nourished and sustained by his own life. Eternal life is man's life committed to the service of God and thereby to the service of the neighbour, a life which certainly also serves him best who is allowed to live it. Eternal life is a strong and no longer weak life; joyous and no longer sad; true and no longer deceitful. Eternal life is man's indestructible life because it comes from God and is sustained by him. It is life everlasting, extending beyond any natural end which now can no longer be death.

Eternal life is the *free gift* of God. It is not the wages, the salary, the compensation, as death is the wages of sin. Eternal life is not our due from God. It is nothing we have earned. It is not a payment for services well done. Eternal life is not the grand total at the bottom of the payslip, as death is on the payslip of sin. For unlike sin, God is no paymaster or employer or cashier ready to settle accounts. God does not settle accounts. God is a very distinguished gentleman whose privilege and enjoyment it is to give freely and to be merciful. Hence he grants eternal life. Hence human life experienced as eternal life is his un-deserved and free gift, his gift of grace.

Remember, this was the outcome of the Easter story, the history of Jesus Christ, just as death as the wages of sin was its beginning. With Christ's resurrection from the dead God's free gift, eternal life, entered the world. He, the dear son, he, the faithful and obedient servant, he who was willing to make our sin his own and to die our death in replacement of us, he, Jesus Christ, was raised from the dead and recalled from the tomb by the Father. He was robed in eternal life. But now remember also, dear brothers and sisters, that God so acted in Jesus Christ in order that we, truly all of us, without exception, may share in this free gift of life eternal. *His* story now becomes *ours*, just as before *ours* became *his*. This was accomplished when the Easter story reached its climax. This was the great 'but' and 'onward' whereby our sin and with it our death was relegated to the past. This was and this is the light mentioned already in the story of creation. 'God said, *Let there be light!* and there was light.' There was light for us all in the story of Easter, in the event of Jesus Christ. There all of us, mankind itself, were made free for eternal life. The Lord is risen! He is risen indeed! In him and with him we, too, are risen indeed. This is not my private opinion. I repeat it after the apostle Paul who never tired of making this claim. I repeat it after the First Letter of John, 'We know that we have passed out of death into life.'

Granted all this, what remains there for us to be done? Only one thing: to perceive, to accept, and to take to heart that this is so. God's free gift is eternal life in Jesus Christ our Lord. Do you know whom we would resemble were we not to perceive and accept this truth? We would resemble a fool who is likely to say these days: spring is not here yet; the cherry trees are not yet in bloom; it is still raining; the cold weather prevails and, who knows, there may even be some more snow. Would such not be the words of a fool? I could even use a more striking illustration. Did you read in the paper recently that two Japanese soldiers were found in the Philippines, who had not yet heard, or did not believe, that the war had ended fourteen years ago? They continue to hide in some jungle and shoot at everybody who dares approach them. Strange people, aren't they? Well, we are such people when we refuse to perceive and to hold true what the Easter message declares to be the meaning of the Easter story. Sin and death are conquered; God's free gift prevails, his gift of eternal life for us all. Shall we not very humbly pay heed to this message? Death—but life! 'Wake up, sleeper, and rise from the dead, that Jesus Christ may be your light!' He, Jesus Christ, who made our history his own and, in a marvellous turn-about, made his wondrous history our own! He in whom the kingdom of the devil is already destroyed! In whom the kingdom of God and of his peace has already come, to us, to you and me, to us all, on the earth and in the whole world! Amen.

O Lord God, our Father through Jesus Christ thy Son in the power of the Holy Spirit!

Give light to our eyes, we beseech thee, that we may see thy light, the brightly shining light of reconciliation! For man's greatest plight is not to see the light in the broad daylight. Take this plight from us, from all the Christians who today celebrate Easter in the right or in the wrong spirit, from all mankind near and far in its ever-present and ever renewed bewilderment and peril!

Bless whatever efforts are made to bear witness to thy name, thy kingdom, and thy will in our church as well as in other churches and Christian communities that are still separated from us! Enlighten the new man now at the head of the Roman Catholic Church! Govern also all honest efforts on the part of civil authorities, administrations, and courts here and in all the corners of the world! Strengthen the teachers in their commitment to the high task of educating the coming generation; the editors and reporters in their sense of responsibility for influencing public opinion; the doctors and nurses in their faithful work of alleviating the pain of those entrusted to their care! Make up by thy comfort, thy counsel, and thy help for our failure to provide for so many of the lonely, the sick, the poor and the perplexed! Show compassion also to all the people of this house and to their loved ones, and let it mightily work in them all!

Into thy hand we commend ourselves and our needs, together with those of the world. In thee we hope. In thee we trust. Thou hast never put to shame thy people when they earnestly called on thee. What thou hast begun, thou shalt bring to fruition. Amen.

BLESSED BE THE LORD

14 June 1959

O Lord our God! Thou findest us gathered here to proclaim and to hear thy word, to call on thee, to praise thee, and to ask from thee what alone is good and wholesome for us and for the world.

Yet how may this truly come to pass? Thou knowest what kind of people we all are, and we know it ourselves. We cannot hide before thee our hardened hearts, our impure thoughts, our inordinate desires. Nor can we deny the troubles they caused and will cause, our errors and transgressions, the many words and deeds that are unpleasing in thy sight and only help to disturb and destroy the peace on earth. Who are we to presume that we in this hour serve thee and effectively help one another?

Our endeavours are vain if thou dost not speak and act in our midst. We utterly rely on thy promise of mercy and compassion that Jesus Christ came into the world to bring good tidings to us, the poor, to proclaim deliverance to us, the captives, and recovering of sight to us, the blind, and to save us sinners. To this promise we cling today. Thou canst do what we cannot do. Thou wilt do it. We believe and we trust that thou shalt do it, not because we are good and strong, but because thou art.

'Our Father . . .'

Blessed be the Lord day by day! He who bears us up is the God of our salvation. PSALM 68.20

MY DEAR BROTHERS AND SISTERS, how can I invite you and even urge you to join with me—or rather not with me but with what the Scripture says—in this hymn of praise, 'Blessed be the Lord day by day'? Do not our thoughts and feelings as a rule take quite a different course? We do not bless the Lord. All of us, myself included, *grumble*.

We grumble like this: 'Pitied and bemoaned be my fate! Good luck has deserted me! I was duped and dumped right where I am, robbed of a fair deal!' Or else: 'Shame on the people around me, for they played tricks on me or let me down! Shame on the bad environment in which I grew up, perhaps even on my parents who failed to care much about me, to bring me up properly, and to show me their love!' Still another complaint: 'How repulsive, contemptible and annoying is this or that fellowman with whom I must daily associate! How I dislike his manners, or rather his lack of them—his behaviour, or rather his misbehaviour!' Or again: 'I could truly pull my hair and slap myself in the face at the thought of a certain dark period or hour in my life when I was thrown off the right track and made to suffer the consequences until this day!'

The grumbling could also spread and stir up well-deserved protest against the individuals who in our time radioactively infest and poison the good, fresh air with their stupid tests, thereby perhaps spelling disaster for all coming generations. Who knows, the disaster may hang over our heads even now, although we are not yet aware of it. Or we might want relentlessly to criticize the four men assembled for a full five weeks at the round table in Geneva. Instead of pronouncing the long expected word of peace and thereby deciding the future of us all they have as yet produced nothing but the same old trite phrases. The same applies, only more so, to their instigators in Moscow,

Washington and Bonn, as well as to the newspapers—the Swiss press prominently among them—for agitating the cold war day-in and day-out. Lastly, mankind itself, in the East as in the West, has its share of the blame. Like a herd of sheep it seems to rush toward the precipice, dragging along all and everything. One or the other among you might quite possibly wish to include Christianity in his protest, the Protestant Churches and the Roman Catholic Church along with their spokesmen who so often howled and still howl with the wolves! Again and again they certainly appear as weak as to have nothing better to offer than stones instead of bread.

Shall I go on? Many more and specific things remain to be said, deplored, and indicted. Perhaps such deep-seated grumbling about this or that or everything would come as a marvellous satisfaction and relief to many. Perhaps—indeed, why not?—our grumbling might to a greater or lesser degree be justified either in part or point by point!

So what? Shall we bravely go on with our mumbling and grumbling? Should I say 'Amen' at this point? Some of you, it might turn out, would be pleased if I did say it now! They would be full of praise, saying, 'Today I truly felt understood. This is exactly how I feel!'

But wait a minute. We are on the wrong track. At issue is not our self-understanding or our mutual understanding. At issue is our common need to understand something entirely different. This is the reason why I am not free to say 'Amen' as yet.

The wholly different message is this: 'Blessed be the Lord day by day!' You notice, don't you, the entirely different ring. It not only sounds different, it *is* different from all our loud or hushed, our justified or unjustified grumbling. Like a mountain peak it towers over our thoughts and our feelings. Like an earth-quake it shakes the territory of our complaints. Like a torrent it breaks through the dikes of our accusations and verdicts, of our criticisms and protests. 'Blessed be the Lord day by day!' Don't think now that this is only my private opinion! If that were at issue, I might as well openly confess that I myself sometimes grumble. I even like to do it, and always for what I think to be good reasons. But we are talking about a much deeper and better insight than all our human opinions, yours and mine, put together. 'Blessed be the Lord day by day!' This is, very simply, the *truth*. It is *above* us, *against* us, but primarily *for* us. The truth begging to shine in our hearts as does the sun in the early morning. When it rises, all the birds begin to chirp and all the flowers stretch towards its light. No one lives from his own opinions, however outstanding and well-founded they may be. Man lives from the truth. This is the truth: 'Blessed be the Lord day by day!' When we join in this praise, we enter the realm of truth—indeed, we already live in the truth. Now the day breaks. Now, and only now, true life begins. Because this is so, I could not say 'Amen' before. Because this is so, I am now bold enough, in spite of all and everything, to invite you, urgently and fervently, to join in. Yes, 'Blessed be the Lord day by day!' Let me briefly explain it to you.

'Blessed be the *Lord*!' The Lord makes truth to be truth, the firm ground on which we can stand and walk, the air which we may breathe. The Lord is the origin and the beginning from which we come; he is also the destiny and end to which we go. He is not only great, but the only great One; not only good, but the only good One, the fountain of all goodness. He is the free Lord, the source of all freedom. He is the only Lord, because he is the creator of all things; because everything belongs to him; because we are all his own.

'*Blessed* be the Lord!' 'To bless' quite simply means 'to let right be right', 'to approve'. And since it is the Lord whom we bless, we are bound to put ourselves in the wrong and disapprove of ourselves. By the way, have you noticed that in all our church hymns the Lord is blessed in one way or another? He is placed in the right, and we are placed in the wrong. We just sang from our Hymnal and shall do so again later in the Service. You see, by this singing we already join in this blessing of the Lord. One thing is essential now, and only one: seriously to ponder what we sing, really to mean it, and then to act accordingly. Whatever this implies, it does not imply the approval of our fate or of our fellowmen, even less of our newspapers or of any political party. This is entirely left to our conscience and our inclinations. Nor does it imply exalting any creature, life itself, or the world, only exalting the Lord. *Him* shall we bless because *he* deserves it—because blessing him is neither an artificial nor a pious gesture, but the most natural, necessary, and self-evident thing to do, because he alone is right, beyond our alleged rights and over against our wrongs. To bless him is good because in so doing we fare well, we land, as the English say, 'on the safe side'. From the world of deceit we journey into the land of truth in which we can live.

Day by day, each morning anew, we are asked to bless the Lord. A great many things cannot be done daily, can they? We cannot work equally well every day or be in good spirits and a pleasant mood. Neither can we, fortunately enough, take life too seriously every day and put on the same sad face. But one thing is a must—every single day, whatever the circumstances, in rain or shine, in cheerful happiness or deepest affliction, in good luck and in bad luck. To bless the Lord, to let him be righteous, is the one great task for each and every day. Why is this so? Because day by day he is the origin from which we come, day by day also the destiny to which we move. Because day by day he is the one great, good and free Lord who grants us freedom. In short, because day by day he is the Lord. He who keeps Israel will neither slumber nor sleep, as another Psalm puts it. He keeps watch over us. He is at work day-in and day-out until the end of time and beyond, unto eternity. Of this we have a small token in our daily blessing of the Lord until we, too, reach our goal.

No one should come afterwards and say: 'He preached today that we *ought* not to grumble, but *ought* to bless the Lord!' We *ought* to? This is not what I have preached. What I have preached is not a law, not a charge, not a chore to which you must submit. If someone joins in the hymn and daily blesses the Lord, he is not in duty bound to accomplish something, like panting uphill in search of an ideal. On the contrary, he will speedily and merrily walk downhill. He may do so, not in some kind of freedom he did or could gain by himself, but in the freedom which springs from the source of all freedom, from him, the one great and free Lord.

He who bears us up is the God of our salvation. In Luther's version, this verse is translated somewhat differently. 'God loads us with a burden, but he also helps us.' This is also very beautiful and true, and thousands upon thousands of people may have found comfort in this wording. I chose to quote the verse from a modern translation. I think it renders even more accurately what the author of the psalm had in mind, and is perhaps even more beautiful and true than Luther's interpretation. After all God does not load us with a burden; we are the burden which he was willing to take upon himself, which he now bears. And his bearing us up certainly includes *his bearing with us*. God might very well find us unbearable, perhaps not least because of our grumbling. Grumbling, we really cast an odd figure. He could very well act accordingly and drop us. Yet he refuses to do so. He is the mighty Lord, ready and strong enough to bear with us, with you and me, and actually bears us.

'He who bears us up is the God of our salvation.' This further implies that he not only bears with us, but that he also carries us *out* of the morass of our foolish and mischievous thoughts and deeds, out of our several afflictions, great and small. He carries us *through* the home-grown jungle of our imaginations and aberrations. He carries us *away*, from the kingdom of death into life eternal. We cannot pull ourselves up by our own boot-straps. How could we? But he bears us up.

'I haven't noticed it yet,' you say? Well there are many things we have not yet noticed and therefore hold untrue even though they are true. Foremost among them is this, 'He who bears us up is the God of our salvation.' *Is!* The text does not say the God who helps us a little, who may be our salvation at some future time, perhaps only in heaven. No, he *is* our salvation. It so happens that God is not content with keeping to himself, far away in heaven, shrouded in some divine mystery. He does not want to be God, except as the God of our salvation. We are speaking here, as I can only briefly indicate, of the God whose son is called, and actually is, Jesus Christ—of the God who in this son has become our equal, has sided with us, taken our place and surrendered himself—of the God who in his son has made us his own children, brothers and sisters of Christ—of the God who is our Father because he calls us to Jesus Christ and incorporates us into his people. Think of Christmas, Good Friday, Easter, Ascension. Think also of the great mystery of Pentecost. It is truly the work of the Holy Spirit when we are grasped and held by the truth that makes us free to bless the Lord. Truly, *he who bears us up is the God of our salvation.*

Before I close I wish to come back once again to the *grumbling* we dealt with in the beginning. What about it now? First of all, the Lord God most certainly bears with us in and over against the great and small matters that rightly or wrongly make us grumble. Furthermore, he most certainly bears with us even when we grumble, although this grumbling is never a good thing, justified as it may be. If we may affirm in our confession of faith, 'I believe in the forgiveness of sin', we may rightly take it to mean, among other things, 'I believe in the forgiveness of my daily grumbling, opposition, and protest.'

But let us assume now that we understand and accept this forgiveness. Let us suppose we make good use of the gift of freedom to bless the Lord, to put him in the right and ourselves in the wrong. What would then be our situation? Would it still be possible and legitimate to go on grumbling as if nothing had happened? The other day I read a strange piece of news about a prince, the brother of the Belgian King. As a city presented him with the gift of a beautiful new rifle, he declined to accept it, explaining, 'I am sorry, I do not know how to shoot.' How would it be if we said very kindly, 'I am sorry, I no longer know how to grumble', instead of unrestrainedly grumbling whenever the urge wells up within us? Or, more cautiously, 'I only know how to grumble a little. To be honest, I do not feel at ease and I am ashamed when I do it. I am really through with it. Thanks for the rifle, anyhow.' Why am I through with it? I am through with it because I have better things to do. Because my grumbling has been superseded by the great truth which is free and sets free: *Blessed be the Lord day by day! He who bears us up is the God of our salvation.* Amen.

Dear heavenly Father! We give thee thanks. Let it truly come to pass that in our hearts and words and deeds we may bless thee as the righteous one day by day. Even today and, through the power of thy Holy Spirit, also tomorrow and after-tomorrow. Bear with us and bear us up, each and everyone of us, as in the past so in the future. We all stand in need of thee, each in his own way. Be with us and remain the God of our salvation for us, for all people in this house, and for our loved ones near and afar!

Be thou and remain the God of salvation above and amidst the perplexities and frustration of human ventures and current events! Tell and show to all people that no one is lost to thy sight, but that no one can escape thee either! Make thyself known everywhere as the Lord of the pious and of the godless, of the wise and of the fools, of the healthy and of the sick! Be thou the Lord of our poor churches, Protestant, Catholic and what else, the Lord of the righteous and of the unrighteous governments, of the well-fed and of the underfed nations, in particular the Lord of all those who feel called today to speak and to write so many good and a great many not so good things. Be thou the protector of us all in whom we may trust, and the judge of us all to whom we shall be responsible on the Last Day, and are responsible already now.

O thou great, holy, and merciful God, we are longing for thy ultimate revelation when every eye shall see that the whole created world with its history, all men and their life histories were, are, and will be in thy good and strong hands. Thanks be to thee that we may joyfully look forward to this great event. All this we ask in the name of Jesus Christ in whom thou hast eternally loved, chosen, and called us. Amen.